Twayne's English Authors Series

Sylvia E. Bowman, *Editor*

INDIANA UNIVERSITY

Augustine Baker

 104

Augustine Baker

By ANTHONY LOW

New York University

Twayne Publishers, Inc. :: New York

FOR
VIRGINIA L. PAINE
AND
JEANIE M. LOW

Preface

Although separated by his Catholicism from the main currents of English literature, Augustine Baker is of interest as the only professional English mystic, in the central tradition of English mysticism, whose writings have survived from the seventeenth century. One must go back to the great English mystics of the fourteenth century—Walter Hilton, Julian of Norwich, and the anonymous author of the *Cloud of Unknowing*—to find a comparable figure. Mystical overtones appear in the writings of the Quakers and other Nonconformists; but, if the orthodox Church of England produced anyone who devoted his whole life to the pursuit of mysticism, his writings have not survived. Yet, if Baker stands alone in his country and time, his writings are still useful to an appreciation of much seventeenth-century English literature. Many writers made use of mystical terminology or imagery, or in some cases wrote from the pressure of actual mystical experience of a lower order. Thus, for example, the poetry of Henry Vaughan and Thomas Traherne, or Francis Quarles, or even parts of Milton's *Il Penseroso*, can better be understood against the background of the mystical tradition.

In the present state of critical awareness, it no longer is necessary to stress the importance of religious writings in the seventeenth century. The work of Helen White (and many others) has amply demonstrated that religious and devotional writings were at the "very center" of literary activity during the period. Therefore, although it would once have seemed eccentric, inclusion of Augustine Baker among the more familiar English writers now requires no apology. Like other relatively minor writers, Baker is read partly for the light he throws on more important figures; but in the field of religious thought he should be read for his own sake. His discussion of the approaches and first stages of mysticism is unsurpassed in its clarity and practicality.

I have not attempted a detailed analysis of Baker's work in this study but a broad general survey. My hope is to encourage readers to turn to Baker himself. Because no good modern life of Baker is available, I have devoted my second chapter to a rather extensive biography, with accompanying critical commentary on the development of his central ideas. Since most of his writings are based on experience, familiarity with his life is helpful in understanding his work. Moreover, Baker's life was more eventful and interesting than one might expect of a man devoted to religion.

Chapter 3 begins with a brief introduction to mysticism and its terminology for readers unfamiliar with the subject. The rest of the chapter examines the general lines of Baker's approach to mysticism. In the succeeding chapters, I have found it fruitful to examine certain key topics in the writings, relating them to the mystical tradition and to the work of other English writers in the period. These topics are his insistence on the precedence of will or love to understanding—and experience to learning—in contemplation and its approaches; his emphasis on inspiration and spiritual freedom; and his adherence to a *via media* of practicality in his approach to the mystical way and to asceticism. These themes can in turn be reduced to the basic question of personal religion on the one hand and of institutional religion on the other.

Students of the period will recognize that the conflict between institutionalism and individualism—a conflict with which, in somewhat different form, we are only too familiar at the present time—was at the root of the religious disputes in England during the sixteenth and seventeenth centuries, combining with economic and political factors to result in the Civil War. The same issue motivated such diverse books, conservative and visionary, as Richard Hooker's *Ecclesiastical Polity* and John Bunyan's *Pilgrim's Progress*. Baker's position with regard to individualism in religion (and he was supported in it by his order) parallels in some respects that of the Puritans and especially the Quakers, necessitating a revision of the conventional simplification that pictures Catholics as wholly on the side of institutionalism during this period.

Sancta Sophia, the book by which Baker is best known, was published in 1657, sixteen years after his death. It has remained in continued use, first by Catholics and more recently by Angli-

Preface

cans, as a devotional guide. Baker intended it for this purpose, much as Bunyan designed *Pilgrim's Progress* not for literary pleasure but for the instruction and comfort of the elect. Unlike Bunyan, Baker has been relatively neglected by literary critics. Although the standard literary histories call him the chief mystical figure in his period, they have treated him briefly. It is hoped that the present study will help to bring him more of the attention he deserves from those interested in seventeenth-century thought.

For what merit this book may have I gratefully acknowledge my debt to Professor Douglas Bush of Harvard University, who introduced me to the subject, and to Professor Herschel Baker, also of Harvard. Sister M. St. Teresa Higgins of Regis College kindly discussed her work on Baker with me and lent me her bibliography before I was able to see her thesis. I am grateful to the libraries at Harvard University and at Boston College for extending me their facilities, and for the considerable help given me by Sister Helen at the interlibrary loan desk of Seattle University. My debt to Abbot Justin McCann will be partly evident in my notes but ought to be mentioned since no study of Baker would be possible without heavy reliance on his critical and textual work. My friend and former colleague Murray Prosky has helped with suggestions and encouragement. Finally, gratitude of another order is due my wife for patiently accepting the long withdrawals from human society that a work of this kind requires. Any faults that remain in the book are my own responsibility.

The Research Committee at Seattle University provided financial assistance for preparing the manuscript. I wish to thank the following publishers for permission to quote from their editions: Burnes & Oates for Knowles's *The English Mystics*, for *English Spiritual Writers*, ed. C. Davis, and for *The Confessions of Fr. Augustine Baker;* the Catholic Record Society for *Memorials of Father Augustine Baker;* E. P. Dutton & Co. for *The Journal of George Fox*, Everyman Edition; and The Newman Press for *The Cloud of Unknowing.*

ANTHONY LOW

New York University

Contents

Chronology

1575　Augustine Baker born December 9 in Abergavenny, Monmouthshire. Attends Free Grammar School of Henry VIII.

1587　February, sent to school at Christ's Hospital, London.

1590　May, matriculation at Broadgates Hall, Oxford.

1592　May, return to Abergavenny, legal studies.

1596　September, at Clifford's Inn.

1596　November, admitted to Inner Temple.

1598　October 7, death of elder brother Richard; summoned home to Abergavenny; appointed Recorder.

1600　Escape from drowning; religious conversion.

1603　May, conversion to Catholicism.

1605　February, departure for the Continent with Thomas Preston.

1605　May 27, received into Benedictine Order at St. Justina's, Padua.

1606　June, illness; return to England. Death of father. London, Buckley affair.

1607　Religious profession.

1608　Cook Hill, Worcestershire, second attempt at prayer. Experience of "passive" contemplation, discouragement, return to London.

1613　Ordained priest at Rheims (date uncertain).

1620　Spring, last visit to Abergavenny. Joined by Leander Pritchard.

1620　May, at house of Philip Fursdon in Devonshire. Third and final conversion to contemplative life.

1621　July, consumption; return to Gray's Inn Lane, London. Antiquarian research.

1624　Spring, at St. Gregory's, Douay, for a few days.

1624　Spring, spiritual adviser of the English Benedictine Nuns at Cambray.

1633   Joins monastic community at St. Gregory's, Douay.

1638   Summer, sent on English mission. London and Holborn; hunted by pursuivants.

1641   August 9, death in London. Buried in St. Andrew's, Holborn.

1657   Publication of *Sancta Sophia* at Douay.

Augustine Baker

CHAPTER 1

Baker as Writer

I Historical Background

MYSTICAL writing was on the rise in Catholic Europe during Augustine Baker's lifetime. Born in 1575, Baker experienced his religious conversion in 1600 and died in 1641. In Spain, St. Teresa (1515–82) died when Baker was seven, and St. John of the Cross (1542–91) when Baker was sixteen. The spiritual revival spread to France, where St. Francis de Sales (1567–1622) and St. Vincent de Paul (c. 1581–1660) were Baker's near contemporaries. If England had remained Catholic—and if such possibilities are worth speculating about—it is likely that Baker would have been only one figure in a general spiritual movement; as matters stood, he remained almost alone.

For largely historical reasons, the Anglican Church was generally hostile to mysticism during this period. When the monastic properties were confiscated under Henry VIII, government propagandists found it necessary to minimize the significance of contemplation and other monastic activities. Contemplatives and mystics were pictured as parasites on society, a view which many Protestants already were disposed to accept and one which lingered long after the dissolution of the monasteries was an accomplished fact. Mystical activity or writing in seventeenth-century England was therefore to be found, for the most part, not among the orthodox members at the center of the Church of England, but on its fringes, or among the Quakers, Nonconformists, and varied religious enthusiasts of the period. Men like George Fox and John Bunyan characterize this spiritual enthusiasm which, if not strictly mystical, still shares some common ground with mysticism.

During the sixteenth century, a general disenchantment with mysticism and other forms of personal religion occurred on the Continent as well as in England. The Reformation, with its attendant enthusiasms—illustrated most strikingly in such side phe-

nomena as the Anabaptist movement—produced a reaction
against mystical thought in the Catholic Church. Ronald Knox
points out that, after the Council of Trent everything in the
Church was standardized and regimented, including prayer and
the spiritual life. Then this natural defensive reaction to Protestantism "led to [a] counter-reaction, and the seventeenth century
became a century of mystics . . . even the exiled Church of England produced, in Father Baker's *Sancta Sophia,* a classic of the
interior life."[1] David Knowles, in agreement with this thesis,
writes concerning Baker: "The decades of his maturity coincided
with the first great wave of what Bremond has called *L'Invasion
mystique,* when the books and first disciples of the great Spanish
and Italian saints were arriving in France and the Low Countries
to kindle new fires and light new lamps there. Of this invasion Fr
Baker was at once a beneficiary and an agent."[2]

Baker, although he can be placed in this widespread movement,
was nevertheless a real originator—an agent, to use Knowles's expression—in furthering and directing it. While mysticism was
playing a growing role in the Church as a whole, it is apparent
from the history of Baker's life that he evolved his belief in its
importance unaided by anyone among the English Benedictines,
whom he was to join. In fact, it appears from the early biographies that he and his disciples were practically alone in the English Congregation in really understanding and valuing the contemplative way. Baker was a moving force within his own circle.
Among his other achievements, he can claim the honor of having
been the instrument that reintroduced the English Benedictines to
the life of contemplative prayer.

II *Baker's Writings*

Most of Baker's voluminous writings fall into two categories:
antiquarian research, chiefly concerned with Benedictine history
before the dissolution of the monasteries, which was distilled for
publication as *Apostolatus Benedictinorum in Anglia* (Douay,
1626); and the numerous spiritual treatises and translations that
were drawn upon by Serenus Cressy for *Sancta Sophia.* Paradoxi-
cally, this book, by which Baker is best known, is a kind of collab-
oration; Baker supplied the raw material and Cressy, as editor,
imposed the final form. Most of Baker's work has remained in
manuscript, and several lists and descriptions of this extant mate-

rial have been made by Dom Justin McCann,[3] whose catalogues list some sixty-eight different items.

A definitive biography of Fr. Baker has not yet appeared. The only full-scale work, by Dom Norbert Sweeney,[4] was written before several early lives of Baker were uncovered. Since then, however, five primary documents on Baker's life have been published. First is an unfinished autobiography to the age of twenty-one (*Memorials,* 3–52). Next are three seventeenth-century biographies by his disciples in the Benedictine Order: Peter Salvin, Serenus Cressy, and Leander Pritchard.[5] The last of these is the most complete, but it omits some material found in the others. Finally, Justin McCann has collected and edited the autobiographical material from Baker's treatise *Secretum, sive Mysticum* under the title *Confessions of Augustine Baker.*[6] The *Confessions* are probably the fullest source of information about Baker's interior life. It can be seen merely from this listing of titles that more is known about Baker than is usually the case with figures of the seventeenth century. The Benedictine habit of keeping records makes his life better documented than that of many more prominent men; we know more about him than any other English Catholic priest in the period, and more than any but a very few seventeenth-century English writers.

Although vast amounts of Baker's manuscript material will probably never be published, enough has appeared in print to make it possible to get a good idea of Baker's work. Some of the printed material has drawbacks, however, that should be recognized. *The Inner Life and the Writings of Dame Gertrude More,*[7] for example, which contains Baker's life of his disciple Dame Gertrude, along with considerable exposition of his theory, is a revision of a revision. Baker's original manuscript was first edited and abridged for publication in the seventeenth century, by Fr. Francis Gascoign; it was then further edited and shortened by Dom Benedict Weld-Blundell.[8] In spite of these recensions, however, the latter is still useful for studying Baker's approach to spiritual direction.

More significantly, *Sancta Sophia* itself, although it is the most important book in the Baker canon, is the product of Serenus Cressy's editing; and the editor's work included not only selection and rearrangement of Baker's ideas, but considerable rewriting. The orderly structure of the book, the arrangement of the ideas, and the prose style are almost wholly Cressy's. According to Justin McCann, "in the most general terms . . . the substance of *Sancta Sophia* is Fr Baker's, whereas the literary form is Fr Cressy's." [9] While Cressy remains faithful to Baker's teachings, rewriting inevitably involves some modification, especially with a difficult subject like mysticism. On the other hand, there is good reason to use *Sancta Sophia* rather than the original treatises, because historically this book has presented Baker to his readers. Since the manuscripts are so lengthy and unorganized, it will continue to do so.

Fortunately, a few of Baker's original writings have also been published, and these offer a basis of comparison, both in style and content, between *Sancta Sophia* and the original materials. The specimens of Baker's original work now in print (all edited by Justin McCann) include the *Autobiography* and selections from the *Treatise of the Mission*,[10] the *Confessions,* the *Commentary on the Cloud*,[11] "Of Finding God Within Our Soul," [12] and, in an article by McCann, several passages from original treatises with parallels from *Sancta Sophia*.[13]

Baker was not a bellettrist. A perusal of his writing quickly confirms his own admission that he learned relatively little in his two years of humanistic study at Oxford. His writing is significant to the study of English literature for its ideas rather than its style. The importance and centrality of religion in the literature of the first part of the seventeenth century can hardly be overstated; as Helen White has stated, "religious writing, far from being a special interest on the periphery of literature, was at the very center." [14] Because Baker was a Catholic and an exile, his work had little direct influence on the mainstream of English literature; but his writings are a significance statement of spiritual and mystical ideas that were in the air during this period, and that can be found, less explicitly stated, in much of the poetry and prose of the age.

Not only was religious meditation important in the literature of the seventeenth century, but English poetry was far more influenced by Continental Catholic thinkers than one might first suppose.[15] There are a number of useful studies concerned with mysticism in the period; one might mention Elbert Thompson, Itrat Husain, Robert Durr, and K. W. Salter.[16] No significant use has yet been made of Baker, however, although he is the only systematic English mystic contemporary with Henry Vaughan and other poets of this time who were influenced by mystical thought.

III *Style*

Since prose style cannot be entirely divorced from content, and since it tends to reveal the author's character and way of thinking, a brief look at Baker's style is called for. Baker himself noted that style is one indication of the genuineness of spiritual writing: "He that is in the love and full actual practice of a thing speaketh with truth and feeling, and his words pierce and take effect. So do not the cold diffident words of them that speak that which they love not, nor do practise, nor do understand well what it is" (*Confessions*, 144–5). Baker's prose is never cold and diffident, but it is occasionally dry. At its worst, it can be pedantic and diffuse.

In the following passage, an example of Baker at his worst, he is explaining that he has decided to write his autobiography, in spite of his distaste for publicizing himself, because the example of God's grace in his life may be helpful to others: "The consideration whereof hath (as I hope) principally moved me to the description of the ensuing life, wherein, I conceive, will appear and be found some of the divine works of grace in the greatest magnificence and measure, as considering the great measure of such impediment as I have specifyed as was in the described soul towards the infusion and receiving of such grace" (*Memorials*, 7). No feeling is shown here for the sound of words, or for the rhythmical structure of the whole; indeed, the legalistic periphrasis makes it difficult to understand him at all. Fortunately, this instance is an extreme one that is not typical of his normal style.

The following is an example of Baker's more elevated style—concrete and vivid in its imagery, rhythmic, touched with his characteristic self-deprecatory humor, and free of pedantry. Characteristically, however, he does not sustain this level for long, and the ending vitiates the effect of the beginning. Baker is writing to his pupils, the nuns of Cambray, about his relapse after his second conversion to the mystical way:

Alack, poor scholar and poor man, what answer shall he herein make to God, to you that have now heard the story, or to his own conscience? You tender hearts and innocent souls, that have not such need or cause for yourselves, weep for him that hath so great cause, but is so hard-

hearted that he cannot weep for himself. It is not the loss of a kingdom
in this world nor any other transitory or base thing that he would weep
or have you to weep for him; but for this that having with incredible
difficulties and mortifications (as before ye have heard) attained to the
case that he had gotten one of his two feet into heaven, and there
might have held and fixed it till he had gotten in the other foot and so
have made an everlasting secure dwelling there, he carelessly suffered
the former foot to be drawn back, or rather drew it back himself and
so lost the fruit of all his former labours, and is very uncertain whether
ever he shall again have the grace to come to the said case or degree,
at least he is sure never to come thither without great labours and difficulties, which whether he shall or no have the grace and strength to
undergo, only God knoweth and in His hands is it to bestow or deny
the same. (*Confessions*, 76–77)

It is plain that Baker, while writing the last sentence, was carried
away by his thoughts and feelings, and the passage lapses toward
the end. Still, the awkward, humorously self-deprecatory picture
of Baker with one foot in heaven is vivid and effective.

The legalisms in Baker's writings, while often pedantic, sometimes have the advantage of accuracy. For example, when he refers to the attempts of his father and brother to obtain him a
benefice, he writes: "For that end, there was a letter written by
one or both of them to the Lord of Abergavenny" (*Memorials*,
48). The phrase "one or both of them," while not elegant, has the
virtue of expressing his knowledge with complete accuracy. A
reader of Baker is soon impressed by his precision: he never blurs
a fact or an idea for the sake of improving his style. While this
accuracy in small details is sometimes almost annoying, it is a convincing reassurance of his trustworthiness. He is not a man given
to exaggeration or embellishment.

Baker's style of writing, then, is reliable and accurate, but lacks
grace. Instead of aiming at good, clear, literary prose, he used
methods and phraseology borrowed from his study of the law.
Legal style is often characterized by the proliferation of modifying and qualifying phrases; this is precisely the style into which
Baker often falls. On a larger scale, it characterizes his treatises as
wholes: they exhibit not symmetrical proportion among their
parts but an attempt to qualify with exactness every idea, no matter how unimportant to the argument. His writing thus becomes
accretive and meandering, and the basic idea is often obscured by

supporting material. According to Justin McCann, perhaps the only man since Cressy to have read all the manuscripts, "The books are, in fact, constructed by the method of addition, rather than on a formal plan with beginning, middle and end, so that they tend to be invertebrate." [17]

In part, Baker's "invertebrate" style was due to the nature of his subject. He had constantly in mind the importance, when writing about spiritual matters, of not stressing one idea at the expense of its opposite. Religion, and especially mysticism, is full of apparent contradictions, involving paradoxes "whose opposition is soluble by experience alone, not by discursive reasoning." [18] Liberty of the soul and obedience to authority, free will and providence, individual initiative and Divine grace—a multitude of paradoxes enter into Baker's teachings. Careful to avoid misunderstanding or misinterpretation, he rarely comments on one element of a paradox without at least mentioning the other. Since his goal was to instruct beginners in the mystical way and to avoid leading them into errors, he denied himself the language of rhetoric and metaphor, as well as the simplicity of unqualified doctrines. As Sister St. Teresa Higgins suggests, it was Baker's aim "to teach, to encourage, and to set souls securely free in the ways of contemplative prayer," not to write artistically. [19]

Thus Baker's first purpose was not literary or even logical coherence, but practical instruction: "Indeed I do not think myself to be much out of my way, or beside my matter, when I express anything, whatsoever it be, that I think may be for your spiritual use, albeit it do not immediately concern the title and matter of my intended book" (*Commentary*, 183). If such intentions sometimes interfere with Baker's style, *Sancta Sophia* and his other works have, at least, the compensating merit of extreme lucidity. Unlike many mystics, Baker is largely intelligible to the nonmystic; and this virtue must count heavily in his favor as far as most readers are concerned.

IV *Sources*

Since mysticism is basically personal and experiential, it may seem contradictory to speak of sources or of a mystical tradition. Nevertheless, well-defined relationships are often perceptible between mystics; and, if the mystical experience itself cannot be passed on, terminology and advice can. Although Baker's personal

experience with prayer gave him the drive to write, and although
he often stated that no one who had not actually lived the mystical life was qualified to write about it, he nevertheless derived his
terms from books. Since he never met a spiritual director who
could help him personally, reading was his only external guide to
the mystical way. Indeed, he may have written treatises to the
nuns of Cambray while he was their spiritual adviser, instead of
simply talking to them, because of the importance the written
word had in his own religious development. Baker received the
final impetus in his conversion to Catholicism from the books in
the library of his brother-in-law, Henry Pritchard; and his third
and successful attack on the contemplative way was also precipi-
tated by his spiritual reading. In both cases, the first impulse came
from an interior call, but he could carry out his mission only by
means of knowledge obtained from books.

In evaluating the relative importance of Baker's sources, we can
be sure that he was thoroughly familiar with and valued highly
those treatises that he went to the trouble of personally translating
or transcribing. According to Justin McCann,[20] Baker almost certainly translated or transcribed the *Cloud of Unknowing;* the
Epistle of Privy Counsel; Richard Rolle's *The Anchor of the
Spirit;* Constantine Barbanson's *The Secret Paths of Divine Love;*
Blosius' *Brevis Regula, Tabella Spiritualis,* and *Consolatio Pusil-
lanimium;* Bonilla's *Pax Animae;* Benet Canfield's *The Rule of
Perfection* (placed on the Index during the Quietist controversy);
Harphius' *Theologica Mystica,* including *The Mirror of Perfec-
tion;* Walter Hilton's *Scale of Perfection;* Tauler's *Sermons* and
Institutes; and Thomas à Kempis' *Soliloquy of the Soul, Valley of
Lilies,* and *The Imitation of Christ.* Baker also translated and fre-
quently referred to a treatise by St. Teresa's spiritual director, *The
Relation of Fr. Balthazar Alvarez, sent to his General, concerning
his Prayer.*

In addition to the authors Baker translated and therefore knew
thoroughly, he shows at least some degree of familiarity with
these mystics and spiritual writers: St. Gregory of Tours, St. Gregory Nazianzen, St. Bernard, Surius, Peter Blomevenna, Michael of
Constance, Alvarez de Pas, Antonio de Rojas, Denis the Carthusian, Ruysbroeck, Joannes a Jesu Maria, Suso, Bellarmine, and St.
Catherine of Siena. He had read the *Little Flowers of St. Francis,*
and he refers to many other writers as well; but there is no cer-

tainty how well he knew them. Most of the literary influences on Baker fall into three groups, in addition to the Bible: the writings of such early Christians as Dionysius or St. Augustine; the late medieval and early Renaissance treatises by the mystics of England and the Low Countries; and the work of Baker's immediate predecessors and contemporaries—St. Teresa, St. John, Constantine Barbanson, Benet Fitch.

Of St. Teresa and St. John of the Cross, who from our perspective appear two of the greatest Catholic mystics, Baker says relatively little; but it should be remembered that they preceded Baker by only a short time. It is evident, however, that Baker read at least part of St. Teresa's *Life* and that he valued her writings highly. He says of her that "she was destined by Him [God] to be the mistress and teacher of true contemplative prayer, then almost unknown to the world." [21] Baker mentions St. John of the Cross a number of times, referring specifically to the *Ascent of Mount Carmel*. Considering that Baker instructed himself in mysticism, and apparently in theology as well, it is surprising that his reading was as systematic and discriminating as it was. He was educated in Protestant schools, and he spent his productive life as a Recusant in England or in exile on the Continent. These were not conditions conducive to leisurely, well-ordered scholarship; but he overcame his difficulties admirably.

CHAPTER 2

Outward Life

AUGUSTINE Baker was characterized in a poem prefacing the 1657 edition of *Sancta Sophia* as "that mysterious Man." [1] The phrase is appropriate, both in the strict religious sense and because he is a difficult man to understand. Because he was primarily a mystic, who felt that internal prayer was the most important part of his life, the center of his efforts and the true extent of his accomplishments are hidden in that "secret life" [2] which was his relation to God in prayer. It is in the nature of a contemplative life that only peripheral aspects can be scrutinized or judged: the effect of a man on others around him, the nature of his actions, or what we can learn from his writings. For this reason, for example, the number and enthusiasm of Baker's converts to Catholicism are significant in a study of his ideas: they are a gauge of his sincerity, —an indication that his principles were not merely theoretical but were successfully put into practice.

Baker was a mystery, also, in the sense that it is difficult to form a final judgment about his character. There are several seemingly equivocal elements in his life. He was a monastic for years but spent little time in monastic community; he profoundly hated controversy but became the center of several serious disputes and continued to be a controversial figure long after his death; he made many convinced friends and disciples but offended most of his religious superiors. Although he is chiefly known for his mystical writings, Professor David Knowles, a recognized authority on English mysticism, has even implied that Baker was not a true mystic at all.[3] Although discussion of this point must be delayed until later, it is enough to say here that although most lives, when carefully examined, reveal conflicts and paradoxes, the life of a man progressing through the stages of contemplative prayer ought to show an increasing unity of purpose and appearance. If the devil's advocate can produce elements which are really (and not just apparently) out of place, then something is wrong.

I *Early Years*

Augustine Baker was born in the Welsh town of Abergavenny on December 9, 1575. His birthplace, the second largest market town in Monmouthshire, was the seat of the barons of Abergavenny, at the time of Baker's birth members of the Neville family, who had technical precedence as the first barons in the kingdom. Baker's father, William, was Steward of the Lordship of Abergavenny, a post which was the more important because the baron was seldom in residence. He was also a justice of the peace, and at one time may have been Sheriff of Monmouthshire.[4] Baker's mother, Maude Lewis, was a daughter of the Vicar of Abergavenny. Both parents were of Welsh descent and Augustine Baker could probably number Owen Glendower among his ancestors.[5]

Father Baker, who took the name Augustine, by which he is usually known, after he joined the Benedictines, was christened David Baker. He was named for his uncle and godfather, David Lewis, a prosperous and successful lawyer. Under Queen Elizabeth, Lewis held the offices of Master of Requests, Master of St. Catherine's Hospital, and sole Judge of the Admiralty. When he died in 1584, he left his nine-year-old godson a house and property, which probably supplied him with an income for the rest of his life.

Augustine Baker was the youngest of thirteen children, all of whom, except the eldest and the youngest, were girls. His family lived in a large house known as Beili Baker, next to one of the town gates. Baker's parents, according to their son's report, were "naturally of very good moral honesty" (*Memorials*, 17); but they had given up their Catholicism and had conformed, more through fear of penalties than from conviction, to the Church of England. The father appears to have been what was called a "church papist": he conformed outwardly and attended the Church of England services on Sundays, but was by inward belief a Catholic—at least insofar as that is possible in someone unwilling for reasons of prudence to receive the sacraments or to stand up for his convictions. He had the habit, Baker tells us, of walking in his garden and praying aloud from Catholic prayerbooks because, Baker reports, there were no Anglican prayerbooks available in English. It is uncertain what he means, since by then three Books of Common Prayer had been published, as well as a number of approved devotional books.[6] Perhaps he refers to the Catholic works on meditation and spirituality which were already widely dispersed in England, both in their original form and in doctored editions put out by Church of England editors; or possibly his father simply used Catholic books as a relatively safe kind of protest.

William Baker told his son that he would have exiled himself to the Continent on Queen Elizabeth's accession and have remained a Catholic if he had not had a family. He had one, however; and his outward conformity gradually led to a weakening of his inward convictions. "In time," Baker writes, "he came to lose all sense of Catholick religion, accommodating himselfe exteriorly . . . and nothing troubled his mind either one way or other concerning Catholicks or Protestants beleif" (*Memorials*, 19). The situation in Baker's family was a common one at that time, for while at first those in favor of abandoning Catholicism for the Established Church were relatively few, the necessity for conforming often led to a gradual acceptance of the new order, in the second or third generation if not in the first, until at length the Catholics were in the minority.

Immediately following Queen Elizabeth's accession to the throne, Parliament had passed the Act of Uniformity, which permitted only one form of worship—one according to the Book of Common Prayer. At the same time, the Oath of Supremacy was required of the bishops and most of the parish priests, as well as of officeholders; this oath involved acknowledging Elizabeth head of the Church and denying all papal authority. All parishioners were required to attend church on Sundays, on pain of a shilling fine. William Baker would also have risked losing his post as steward if he had not attended services.

In 1563, the penalties for refusing to take the Oath of Supremacy or for defending the papal supremacy were increased to confiscation of all property and life imprisonment for the first offense, and a traitor's death for the second. Then in 1570, Pope Pius V issued the bull *Regnans in Excelsis,* which excommunicated Elizabeth as a heretic and released her subjects from allegiance to her. This unfortunate document was a disaster to the English Catholics who were, with very few exceptions, loyal Englishmen; and most of them, by this time at least, had no desire to stage a violent political revolution. The possibility of an invasion from the Continent, which reached its height in 1588, also made the position of the English Catholics difficult and provided political justification for their persecution. In 1571, it was made treasonable to bring Papal bulls, religious medals, rosaries, or anything blessed by the Pope into England. In 1585, after it became apparent that the missionary priests trained on the Continent were succeeding too well in keeping Catholicism alive in the country, it was declared treason for any priest ordained abroad to return to England, or for anyone to give such a priest shelter.

The penalties against Catholics were not enforced uniformly, but were used partly as threats, though heavy fines were commonly levied. Between 1577 and 1603, 183 Catholics were executed, including 123 priests,[7] and perhaps three hundred more may have died in prison. Priests, the figures reveal, ran a much greater risk of death than laymen, so that Baker, after his ordination, took the chance of being arrested as a traitor as long as he remained in England. During his stay in London between 1607 and 1624, he was twice briefly imprisoned, and his library was robbed by pursuivants. "With one of them, who knew him better than the rest, he was forced to make a bargain or composition for the future, that every time he met him and might lay hands on him, if he would, he should give him 20 shilings, and so be quitte" (*Memorials*, 100). Pursuivants were men empowered to arrest and transport offenders across county lines; in practice, however, they sometimes resembled bounty hunters.

When James I came to the throne in 1603, he at first adopted a propitiatory attitude toward the Catholics to gain their support. Parliament, however, which had many Puritan members, actually increased the penalties against Catholicism, and the persecution soon resumed. It was now, however, more erratic. During the negotiations with Spain for the marriage of Prince Charles and the Infanta, the government relaxed the attack; when these negotiations were broken off, persecution resumed. Similarly, negotiations with the French led several times to lax enforcement of the penal laws, although the laws themselves remained. Twenty-eight Catholics were executed during this period, including nineteen priests.[8] In the period immediately preceding the Civil War, persecution increased once more, and Baker's last years in England were precarious. In Wales, where Baker grew up, the situation was much the same, except that Catholicism held on longer, partly because it was associated with Welsh nationalism. Nevertheless, when Baker returned to Abergavenny as a Catholic, he was told that some of his childhood friends, now in positions of authority, were trying to have him arrested (*Memorials*, 100).

Baker spent his childhood in Abergavenny where he attended the Free Grammar School of Henry VIII (whose chief contribution to the school had been to take most of its endowment when he dissolved the monasteries). When Baker was eleven, his father decided to send him to boarding school because the Grammar School could offer him nothing more academically; and his father, determined to push his son ahead in the world, wanted him to learn to speak English without a provincial accent. The first language of Baker's district was Welsh, and he had learned English "very imperfectly, especially as to the right pronunciation of it." Anyone who sought preferment was well advised to be "brought up . . . in those places of England, where good English is spoken" (*Memorials*, 30).

For these prudent reasons, Baker was entered in Christ's Hospital in London. He remained there for three years—except for a two-month holiday which he enjoyed in the fall of 1588 on account of the threatened invasion by the Spanish Armada. He notes in his autobiography that, when he arrived in the city on February 8, 1587, he was met by bonfires in the streets and by great public rejoicing: it was the day on which Mary Queen of Scots was executed at Fotheringay. The Master of Christ's Hospital, Ralph Waddington, proved to be a "zealous Protestant" who made the students read a chapter of the English Bible every day and say evening prayers from the Book of Common Prayer. On Sundays, the boys were taken to church to "hear the common service both morning and evening with severall sermons at those two times, besides the singing of psalms" (*Memorials*, 32–33). Everyone was required to write summaries of the sermons for inspection by Dr. Waddington. On the whole, Baker felt that his stay at Christ's Hospital was beneficial for his academic learning, his knowledge of Christianity, and his pronunciation of English. Despite the Sunday sermons, his memories of school were pleasant.

In the spring of 1590, at the age of fourteen, Baker entered

Broadgates Hall, Oxford (later Pembroke College). His tutor was a relative, William Pritchard, a "zealous Protestant" but "anti-Puritan," and also a humanist and a "meetly good Ciceronian" (*Memorials*, 40–41). Baker, however, soon fell into unfortunate company among the students. Securing a release from the authority of his tutor, he ceased studying, spent his money on treating his friends to feasts, was "daily and nightly abroad" (*Memorials*, 43), and neglected his work. His natural inclinations restrained him from drinking or getting into serious trouble; and, although he speaks of his youthful sins with a remorse like St. Augustine's, his most significant fault was probably neglect of his studies. After about two years at Oxford, he left in May, 1592, without taking a degree, and went home to Abergavenny.

II *Legal Training and Worldly Plans*

For the next four years Baker lived at Beili Baker, where he studied Law French and elementary law. He read, mainly on his own, a number of legal books which his older brother Richard, a counselor-at-law, lent him. At the same time, he later reported, his sense of religion was decaying and "tending more to a certain atheism" (*Memorials*, 46). These years saw two attempts by his father to settle him in life. First came an effort to marry him to an heiress, then a plan to get him a benefice through the patronage of the Lord of Abergavenny; but both schemes failed. Baker's loss of the benefice came about through an amusing circumstance: as he was too young to be inducted into it immediately, another man took it temporarily in his place; but, when the time came, he simply refused to resign, and nothing could be done to remove him. Baker was later to ascribe the failure of these plans to providence, for either marriage or benefice would have totally changed his subsequent life.

He returned to London in the fall of 1596 to continue his legal studies. After a month at Clifford's Inn, he entered the Inner Temple in November, the usual time of admittance.[9] Since he was more diligent in his legal studies than he had been at Oxford, he was later to become a very competent solicitor. During this stay in London (1596–99), he frequently went to the theater. According to Pritchard, his "recreation was to resort to playes; whither yet he never went without a pocket book of the law, which he did read when the play or any sort of it pleased him not" (*Memorials*, 66).

Unfortunately, Baker's detailed autobiography breaks off before this period; and we are not informed what plays he saw, or whether any were Shakespeare's.

After he had spent two years at the Inner Temple, on October 7, 1598, his brother Richard died; and Baker was summoned home. Since his father's ambitions for the older son had been frustrated by death, he now began to press harder the advancement of the younger. "His eldest brother being dead," Pritchard writes, "the father came to affect this son more tenderly, and to require of him that he should be more frequently at home, and delighted to spend more time in company and discourse with him, imparting to him his own knowledg and experiences, and imploying him in his affairs" (*Memorials,* 71). Baker must have felt mixed emotions in these circumstances, since, in effect, he owed this new affection and interest to his brother's death, and to the principle of primogeniture.

Now his father's favorite, Baker could look forward to a distinguished career, helped forward by every influence his father could command. William Baker soon got his son the office of Recorder of Abergavenny, which the older brother had held. Baker was to spend the next five or six years living in Abergavenny, studying the law, and making occasional trips to London on business. He had by this time gradually drifted away from religion, having, he says, to all intents and purposes become an atheist. His spiritual state during these years is revealed by his confession that at the deathbed of his brother, when his sisters asked him to say the Lord's Prayer, he was unable to remember the words.

III *Conversion*

The first turning point in Baker's spiritual life came about 1600, when he was riding back to Abergavenny from an outlying law court, preoccupied with thoughts about legal business. When he came to one of the rivers near the town, probably the Monnow or the Usk,[10] it was in flood from rains in the hills. His unguided horse, instead of crossing at the ford, started to go over a footbridge, which happened to be rather wide at the point of entrance but narrowed over the river. Baker, unconscious what was happening, was suddenly made aware of his position when the horse balked and began to neigh and tremble. It was now unable to go either forward or back; and, because the bridge was so high, "to leap down was undoubtedly the breaking of the horses neck and of his riders. . . . To devise an escape was vain; nay to think much of anything was not then time." In this emergency, Baker's thoughts turned naturally enough to God; and he made a resolution: "*If ever I git out of this danger, I will beleive there is a God, who hath more care of my life and safty, then I have had of his service and worshipe.*" The next minute, horse and rider were safe on the bank: "He found it done; but how it was done, he could never imagin. And as when he was in danger, he conceived it impossible to escape; so when it was done, he could not imagin but that it was supernaturally done" (*Memorials, 72*).

Whether of supernatural origin or not, this incident had a marked effect on Baker's life: thereafter, he was determined to believe in God and to serve him. At first, he could not decide which kind of Christianity in England represented the true church, but he now grew interested in hearing the arguments of the various factions, whereas previously he had ignored them all.

Several things attracted Baker to Catholicism: his father's use of Catholic devotional books, the fact that his mother and sister were still privately Catholics, his father's statement that he would not have abandoned his old religion had he been free of family responsibilities. In addition, his brother Richard had been present at the disputation in the tower between the Jesuit priest Edmund Campion and the Protestant ministers, just before Campion's execution; and Baker was deeply impressed by this story. Probably, however, the most important of these external influences was the library of his brother-in-law, Henry Pritchard, a Catholic lawyer who had been disbarred for his religion. He had many Catholic books of controversy, and Baker grew more and more interested as he read them. He even went about London publicly inquiring for Catholic apologetics in the bookshops, a very risky proceeding in those years. Finally, in May, 1603, three years after his escape from drowning first interested him in religious matters, he became a Roman Catholic. He made his profession to Richard Floyd, a secular priest. At this time also, and in the next few years, according to Pritchard, he converted "very many" others (*Memorials,* 79).

After Baker became a Catholic, he began to lose interest in the worldly course his father was setting for him. Although his confessor told him that his conscience could rest easy if he continued to earn honest money at the law, giving the excess to the needy, a desire grew in him to leave the world and become a monastic. Since there were then no missionary priests in the area, he did not know whom to see about his plans. At length, in January 1605, he went to London, on the pretense of legal business, but with the intention of crossing to the Continent in order to become a religious. In London he met two English Benedictines belonging to the Italian Congregation.

The Benedictine Rule appealed to Baker, although the records do not reveal whether he had thought much previously about what order to join. Of the various religious orders, "he found himselfe to be fittest for one of a moderate rigor, and which sought God by solitude, retirednesse and contemplation. And he found no propension in himselfe to those of great or extreme rigor, nor to the others which are active" (*Memorials*, 82). From the very first, in fact, he sought a life which combined spirituality and contemplation with moderation and restraint. The Benedictine Rule offered in monastic life a *via media* which appealed to him and which proved to be well suited to his character. He made his decision; and in February, 1605 he went to Dover, accompanied by Dom Thomas Preston, one of the Benedictines. There, after writing his intentions to his father, he took ship for the Continent.

IV   *Italy and London: The Years of Search*

The two Englishmen continued by land, arriving on April 29 at St. Benedict's monastery in Mantua, where a General Chapter or meeting of the Italian Benedictines was in progress. After some discussion, Baker was accepted into the community of St. Justina's in Padua. He took the habit there on May 27, 1605, at the age of thirty. Although he was well treated physically in his new life (he was offered twenty kinds of wine in order to find one that suited his health), he received almost no spiritual instruction. He started on a course of mental prayer, but gave it up after three weeks because there was no one to tell him about perseverance in spite of spiritual dryness. This experience was the first of several when lack of advice was to set him back, and one of many indications how badly his own later writings on contemplation were needed to advise other beginners in prayer. St. Justina's was a reform monastery,[11] but Baker nevertheless was unable to get proper spiritual advice there.

Since life in St. Justina's was pleasant, he developed a love for his monastery and for the Italian countryside. The other monks, mostly the younger sons of Italian gentlemen, quarreled rather noisily with one another, but got on well with the new postulant. Among other things, they taught him how to wash his linen, "with which point of laundry he was unacquainted" (*Memorials*, 85). He settled into a pleasant round of ritual and routine, but stopped praying internally. The change in climate and way of life, however, began to affect his health; and finally his superiors decided he must leave the monastery to return to England, as there seemed no other way of curing him. His new life was too much for his constitution. It is not clear when or why his health grew so precarious, although in the autobiography he halfheartedly attributes it to his misdeeds in college; but he seems to have suffered from chronic illnesses throughout his adult life. Much of the time he was in considerable pain and weakness.

This occasion was the first of several when his health deteriorated so badly that he was forced to move in order to recover. His case was a common one at that time. M. D. R. Leys, commenting on the forced return of William Allen, the founder of the English Seminary at Douay, from the Low Countries to England in 1562 on account of his health, writes: "It is surprising how often during the sixteenth and seventeenth centuries Catholics left the safety of their refuges on the continent to go back, for their health's sake, to their native land, though death was the penalty for their return." [12] Recusants who returned from abroad were eyed with doubled suspicion by the government and its agents.

About a year after Baker's admission to St. Justina's, he left Padua, provided with recommendations and testimonials of noviceship in case his health permitted him to join a monastery elsewhere. He traveled first to Venice, then to Milan. Having sufficient money and leisure, he began the journey slowly, in order to see the country and the people; but something within him urged him to hurry, so he posted to London without delay. There he heard news that his father was ill.

When Baker arrived at Abergavenny, he found his father dying and very glad to see his son again. The father, who was in great pain, prayed continually and gave thanks to God, so that Baker was reminded of Job. When he asked his father if he wanted to be reconciled to the Catholic Church, he found him ready to return without persuasion. He received the sacraments and a few days later he died. Baker played a better part at his father's deathbed than he had at his brother's. He now returned to London to settle his affairs and to sell the land his father had left him; for it was liable to confiscation at any time. His mother and sisters were well taken care of, and Baker had sufficient income to maintain himself, as well as to pay for the antiquarian research that he subsequently undertook on behalf of the English Benedictines.

About this time, two English monks of the Italian Congregation were in London, working on a project for reviving the English Benedictine Congregation. It happened that one old monk of the Marian Benedictines, Fr. Sigebert Buckley, was still alive. Buckley, a member of the community at Westminster Abbey under Queen Mary and Cardinal Pole, had spent half of Elizabeth's reign in prison. Released by James in 1603, he was now in his eighties.[13] The Benedictine Fathers planned to ask Fr. Buckley to aggregate new members into the old congregation, of which he was the only survivor. In this way, the legal continuity of the English Congregation would be preserved. Although Baker did not originate the idea, he was soon involved in the project, taking over the legal business. He now began the first of his antiquarian researches, investigating the history of the Benedictines in England. In November 1607, Robert Sadler and Edward Maihew, two monks of the Italian Benedictine Congregation, were formally aggregated into the pre-Reformation congregation. Baker himself did not join it until later, probably in 1609.[14] About this time, however, he made his formal profession as a Benedictine in the Italian Congregation.

After he completed the legal business in connection with the aggregation, Baker felt a strong urge to retire from the world for a while. He spent some time in London, living in retirement with the Catholic son of Lord Treasurer Buckhurst. When this arrangement proved unsatisfactory, Baker went as chaplain to the house of Sir Nicholas Fortescue in Worcestershire, probably in the spring of 1608. During his stay here he resumed the attempt to live a life of interior prayer which he had begun and broken off in Padua. His health was particularly bad at this time; he was able to eat only a minimum of food, sufficient to keep him alive, and experience proved that, if he ate any more, it would probably kill him.

His appetite, however, was still normal, so he suffered from terrible hunger immediately after finishing a meal.

To this enforced mortification Baker ascribed his rapid progress in his interior prayer. He advanced continually, until at the end of sixteen months he was rewarded with a single experience of what he called passive contemplation. Although this one short experience had a permanent effect on his life and character, it was followed by a repetition of what had happened in Italy: once more he experienced the desolation that is inevitable in contemplative prayer, but this time on a much higher level. He still had no one to advise him or encourage him to persist, and he mistakenly discontinued his attempts to pray, thinking that his discouragement was a sign to do so. For the next twelve years he abandoned contemplative prayer.

Baker lived an outwardly good life during this period, one that would be considered exemplary in an ordinary man. He made some converts to Catholicism, he supported two young men at Louvain who became priests and were martyred on the English mission, and he used his legal knowledge to help widows and needy people and to advise the Benedictines in London. But he suffered from a continuous sense of guilt in spite of his good deeds, for he felt obscurely that he was not living the life he was meant to live. At some time during this period, possibly in 1613 (when he was on the Continent), he was ordained a priest at Rheims. He thought this ordination might supply him with the grace necessary to give his life a sense of inner purpose; but, of course, it did not. He was a man whose potentialities could be fulfilled only by a life of interior prayer; there was no substitute. In these years, therefore, he could find no essential rest. "For," writes Cressy, "being mindful from whence he was fallen, he thought himself in some sort a Cain wandering from the face and presence of God" (*Life,* 85).

Toward the end of this period, in the course of his reading, Baker gained some additional theoretical knowledge of contemplation; and he resolved to make a third assault on the interior life. He was obliged, however, to stay in London for a while; for, in the summer of 1619, the Pope officially restored the English Benedictine Congregation, confirming the steps taken in 1607 by Baker and the Italian monks. Baker was the first in England to submit to the Union of English Benedictines. His new Superior was Fr. Vincent Sadler, and his nominal community, which he was never to see, was Dieulward in Lorraine (now Ampleforth).

V Final Conversion

In the spring of 1620, his business completed, Baker went for the last time to Abergavenny to take leave of his family and friends. Leander Pritchard, a relative, later to become his disciple and first biographer, joined him there. After they had returned to London, Baker, in the company of Fr. Vincent Sadler, left for the West of England, to find a place of solitude where he could retire. On the advice of his superior, he stayed in Devonshire at the house of Philip Fursdon. Here, after three weeks of hesitation, and a strong temptation to continue leading a busy, practical life filled with good deeds, Baker embarked for the third time on a spiritual course; and this time he persevered until his death.

Baker and his biographers call this his "third conversion." The first, in Padua at the age of thirty, lasted only a very short time; the second began in London, at the age of thirty-two, and continued at Cook Hill, Worcestershire, for some sixteen months. The third and last conversion, which he now underwent at the age of forty-five, was the real beginning of his productive life. The difficulties involved in beginning a new life at this age, and of persevering in it, overcoming the habits of a lifetime, can easily be imagined; and they indicate the strength of his resolution. As Baker himself points out, the older a man is when he enters a spiritual life, the harder his task (*Confessions*, 12–28). Baker had finally, however, learned the lesson of perseverance. He had learned, through many years of trial and error, what a good director could easily have told him in the first place. Perhaps this practical experience of the pitfalls in the contemplative way had its uses, since it later enabled him to advise others so well. Although he did not yet know it, his mission from the time of this last conversion was, in effect, to give to others the advice and counsel he had lacked.

Baker remained in Devonshire for a little over a year, faithful to his rededication to internal prayer. During this time he made a number of converts, including his host's son, Cuthbert Fursdon,[15] and Fr. Vincent Sadler's errant nephew, both of whom became priests. The way Baker obtained these conversions is interesting.

According to Cressy, they were converted not by "eagerness to dispute, no, nor so much as any direct inducing or persuading them, but only the giving of a good example, full of modesty and void of all singularity, etc.; but principally by praying for them, and inviting or instructing them how to pray with a sincere resignation to obey the truth, when God should reveal it to them." Baker's policy was to advise non-Catholics who came to him for advice to seek illumination directly from God by means of prayer. He was convinced that anyone who prayed to God "with pure submission of soul and indifferency" would be led to the truth more surely than by human arguments (Cressy, 91, 93). This approach was rare in an age of dispute and polemic, but it worked.

One incident illustrates Baker's method. There was an old woman in the house, a Protestant, with whom every priest who passed through used to hold long debates, attempting her conversion. These arguments only served, however, to antagonize her. Baker left her strictly alone, until at length she asked him why he had not tried to convert her, since she was sure he desired it as much as the others. He answered that he did not believe in using argument or moral force, but that, if she wanted to discover the truth, she could do it by sincere and disinterested mental prayer directly to God. She followed this advice, and in a short while was convinced and became a Catholic. It may be argued that this method is merely a subtler form of moral suasion; perhaps it is, but it seems to violate no one's freedom. The incident illustrates well Baker's conviction that the human soul should be free of outward influence or coercion, that it should approach God as directly as it can, in its own way, without limiting itself to complicated forms of prayer suggested by others. Freedom of the individual nature, a recurring topic in Baker's writings, is further considered in later chapters.

VI *Antiquarian Research*

During his stay with the Fursdons, Baker fell ill of consumption, and again neared death. Therefore, in the summer of 1621 he decided to return to London. He took up lodgings in Gray's Inn Lane, where his health improved once more. He was now plunged more than ever before into business and practical affairs. A book, *Examen Trophaeorum*, by a Cluniac Benedictine, Dom John Barnes, published on the Continent in 1622, questioned whether there had ever been a true English Benedictine Congregation and so threw doubt on the legitimacy of the new Union. Baker, who became the spokesman for the English Congregation in answering these charges, approached the antiquarian John Selden about refuting Barnes; and Selden in turn spoke to Sir Henry Montagu, the Lord Treasurer. Selden would himself have undertaken the refutation had not Baker taken it in hand. Curiously, although the English government had earlier done its best to prove that everything Catholic was inspired and controlled from abroad, the idea that the English Benedictines had been under foreign jurisdiction aroused the indignation of the Anglicans who heard of it, which may explain why Baker was accorded every facility for his researches, even to examining the records in the Tower. Baker's freedom in conducting his research has usually been ascribed to religious toleration among scholars, but it seems to have had the unofficial approval of the government.

Baker made use of Sir Robert Cotton's library, examined a number of state and church documents, and traveled into the country looking for manuscripts. During his researches he met and became friends with many of the English antiquaries of the period. Anthony Wood writes in *Athenae Oxonienses* (1721) that Baker was assisted in his researches "by the learned *Cambden, Sir Rob. Cotton,* Sir *Hen. Spelman,* Mr. *Joh. Selden,* and *Dr. Fr. Godwin* Bishop of *Hereford*: to all whom he was most familiarly known." [16] The product of Baker's researches was published at Douay as *Apostolatus Benedictinorum in Anglia* (1626). This book was compiled and edited by Fr. Leander Jones, who acted as Baker's amanuensis. Fr. Clement Reyner, who is named as author on the title page and is still usually referred to in that role, had little or nothing to do with the book but was honored because of his rank in the religious order. Baker was responsible for almost everything in the book; indeed he also produced six large folio volumes of documentary material, intended for use in a fuller work to be published later, but which he never had the opportunity to finish. Four of the folios are now in the library at Jesus College, Oxford.

In spite of the activities that filled Baker's life during this period, it was entirely different in one respect from the previous period of London activity. He persevered, this time, in prayer; and his enforced business no longer distracted him from the interior life. If Baker had died in 1624, his life would have been chiefly remarkable (or unremarkable) for the part he had played in the revival of the English Congregation. He had come forward three times at crucial points in the re-establishment of the English Benedictines. The first was when he carried out the legal and historical work in connection with Sigebert Buckley. His assistance ensured that the groundwork of the Congregation was well laid. The second was in 1619, when Pope Paul V restored the Congregation, and Baker was the first to accept the Union.[17] The third was when he carried out the antiquarian work just discussed, in the years 1621–24, meeting the attack on the Union and successfully defending it.

VII *Cambray*

It is remarkable that, although Baker was to be remembered chiefly as a mystic, he wrote nothing about mysticism before 1624. In that year the negotiations for the marriage of the Prince of Wales and the Infanta of Spain fell through, and intensified persecution of Catholics was expected. Because of this situation, "fearing the distraction that would result from the threatened persecution" (*Inner Life*, 20), and in obedience to what he felt to be a special inspiration, Baker resolved to accept an invitation from Dom Rudisind Barlow, then the President of the English Congregation, to return to the Continent. He sailed for the Low Countries, probably in May, and arrived in Douay where he was well received at the Benedictine monastery by Fr. Rudisind. Baker had been at Douay for only a short time, however, when Fr. Rudisind asked him to go to Cambray, where a spiritual adviser was needed for the English Benedictine convent which had been established there half a year earlier. Baker, accepting the appointment, proceeded to his new post.

He remained at Cambray for nine years, from 1624 to 1633. During this period, probably the happiest of his life, he spent most of his time in his cell, engaged in prayer, study, and the composition of a number of works on the spiritual life. His writings were educational in purpose, directed toward the small, specific audience of the Cambray nuns, who consisted, on Baker's arrival, of nine postulants, three lay sisters, and three professed nuns, who had been temporarily transferred from Brussels to train the novices. During the period 1625–33, while Baker was at Cam-

bray, twenty-five more novices entered the convent, of whom
about six subsequently left. There was also a regular chaplain and
confessor so that Baker was free of routine duties.[18]

Everything he wrote was intended for the spiritual development of the nuns. Since most of them read English more easily
than Latin, Baker decided to translate a number of mystical works
which he thought would be of value to them: Ruysbroeck, Tauler,
Rolle, Hilton, a Kempis, the *Cloud of Unknowing*. It is evident
from the list of translations that he prized the earlier English mystics and knew them well. He intended to see that his charges got
that instruction about the interior life which he had so unfortunately failed to receive at Padua. His anxiety that the novices
should lack nothing in their spiritual instruction and the shortage
of good books in English on the mystical life are both apparent in
a letter he wrote to his former acquaintance, Sir Robert Cotton, in
1629, begging for books for the nuns:

Their lives being contemplative, the comon Bookes of the worlde are
not for their purpose, and litle or nothing is in thes daies printed in
English that is proper for them. There were manie good English bookes
in olde time, wereof, thoughe they have some, yet they want manie;
and thereuppon I am in their behallf become an humble suitor unto
you to bestowe on them such bookes as you please, either manuscript
or printed, being in English, conteining contemplation, Saints Lives, or
other devotions. Hampole's works are proper for them. I wishe I had
Hiltons Scala Perfectionis in Latin; it woulde helpe the understanding
of the English (and some of them understande Latin). The favour you
shall do them heerin will be had in memorie, both towardes you and
your posteritie.[19]

In order to round out the library at Cambray, if treatises on
particular points were unavailable, Baker wrote them himself. He
discussed problems of prayer, the best methods of spiritual direction, the Benedictine Rule, and other topics. Most of his work,
however, was concerned with the first stages of the interior life—
with the approaches to contemplative prayer. He wrote dozens of
treatises, including most of those "more than forty" [20] that Cressy
used when he compiled *Sancta Sophia*. Because Baker wrote each
treatise as the need for it arose, the manuscripts tend to be somewhat repetitive and unorganized. Baker himself never thought of
writing a popular or general work on spirituality. In the *Commen-*

tary on the Cloud, after remarking that books on mysticism are not meant for the generality of readers, he says: "It may be questioned whether they be fit at all to be printed and published" (152).

Because the audience for Baker's spiritual treatises was extremely limited, his writing lacked the polish an author might give to a work meant for general circulation. At the same time, however, his work derived many of its virtues from this same audience; for his contact with the nuns of Cambray gave him the practical materials for his treatises. Answering their problems and observing their progress, he obtained empirical knowledge of the interior life with which to supplement his reading and his own experience. All genuine mystical writing must probably be experiential; and Baker's personal life, through the long years of conversion, relapse, and final conversion, had given him invaluable knowledge of the problems of the beginner in contemplation. At Cambray, he had other beginners to work with; and, as a result, he produced treatises on the first approaches to contemplation which are unsurpassed in their practicality.

Baker gained a number of disciples among the nuns, the most important of whom were Dame Catherine Gascoigne, the Abbess; and Dame Gertrude More, a daughter of the founder of Cambray, Cresacre More, and a descendant of St. Thomas More. Not all went well at Cambray, however. A division of opinion slowly appeared in the convent, in spite of or perhaps because of Baker's success with some of the nuns; and two groups emerged, one of enthusiatic converts to the contemplative way, and another opposed to Baker's teaching, or, as it came to be called, Bakerism. When a new chaplain, Fr. Francis Hull, arrived at Cambray, he became the focal point of the resistance to Baker. Fr. Francis, although he seems to have been a good man, did not understand mysticism.

Baker, inclined by nature to quietness and solitude, thought that all monastics should follow the contemplative way as far as they could. At the least, those called to contemplation should not be interfered with. Fr. Hull, of a more active temperament, applied to the nuns methods Baker believed to be suitable only for active lay people—frequent examinations of conscience, formal and complicated meditations, conferences, and regular use of the *Spiritual Exercises*. What Baker was combatting, actually, was not clerical worldliness but the misapplication of another kind of spirituality. Baker's teachings were in the contemplative tradition of Rolle and Hilton and the *Cloud of Unknowing*. His work represented, however, only one current in the religious life of the period.

The dominant influence on Catholic spirituality in his time was undoubtedly the Ignatian method. The influence of St. Ignatius Loyola was so great in the Catholic Church of the period that there was some danger of losing sight of other approaches to spirituality. St. Ignatius' *Spiritual Exercises* answered a deeply felt need for depth, interior meaning, and conviction in religion. The Protestant Reformation had, in part, been made possible by the widespread craving for an inner spirituality to supplement or replace what seemed to be the externalization or ritualization of religion. While Protestantism replaced or modified the Catholic framework, the new Catholic spirituality, represented most actively by St. Ignatius, gave it new life from within. But the very success of the Ignatian method carried with it the dangers of overenthusiasm and misapplication. In the hands of men like Fr. Hull, who was, after all, not a Jesuit but a Benedictine, the *Spiritual Exercises* became mechanical and were sometimes applied indiscriminately or against the best interests of the individual. St. Ignatius himself had called for flexibility and common sense in using the *Spiritual Exercises,* and for this reason they were supposed to be used in retreats under experienced directors.[21]

Fr. Hull followed a system of rigid direction and of mechanical application of prescribed methods to all his charges, regardless of differences in character or situation. Baker, on the contrary, believed in encouraging each individual to seek divine guidance directly—to follow, within the bounds of revelation and obedience, an individual path. The conflict between Baker and Hull came to a head in 1633, when the argument was brought before a General Chapter of the English Congregation. Fr. Hull said that Baker's teachings subverted proper authority and that they verged on illuminism. The two charges are related: Hull felt that Baker encouraged his disciples to obey an inner voice and therefore to disobey their superiors—although, in fact, the Mother Superior was Dame Catherine Gascoigne, one of Baker's followers.

The verdict of the chapter was to approve Baker's statement of his teachings and to give, after a careful examination, full approval to all his writings. The conflict had been a matter of misunderstanding and the clash of personalities, possibly fueled by occasional abuses or unconsidered statements by Baker's partisans. Fr. Hull, on his deathbed in 1645, said that he had never opposed Baker or his doctrine directly, but only the abuses of some "pretended practisers of it." In fact, a later Abbess of Cambray wrote that Fr. Hull himself subsequently tried to follow Baker's methods of prayer and direction (Salvin and Cressy, *Lives*, 28, xxxii).

VIII *Douay*

In spite of Baker's exoneration, feelings had run too high for a return to the *status quo ante,* so both Baker and his adversary were transferred from Cambray. Baker returned to St. Gregory's, Douay, where he remained five years, until 1638. At Douay, he continued writing treatises which, however, differed somewhat from those he had written at Cambray. According to Dom Pritchard, "those of Cambray (for the most part) were institutions or canons of a contemplative life; these of Doway, though they also treate of contemplation, yet proceed and insist much upon proving, reasoning, and arguing; and are much of that kind of writing which is called dissertation" (*Memorials,* 122). This difference in method was probably due to the difference in audience. Sister St. Teresa Higgins suggests that the Cambray treatises owe their nature to the fact that they are addressed to a group of women, while those written at Douay are addressed to men. For this reason, the Douay treatises appeal to the intellect and make use of logic and close reasoning, while the Cambray treatises "are clearly aimed at gaining the will." [22]

Baker's life at Douay was, for the most part, quiet and outwardly routine. Since his health was poor, he spent his time chiefly in his cell, where he read, wrote, said his office and the Psalms, and prayed. According to Pritchard, he slept hardly at all; he spent his nights in prayer. He developed the habit of making an immediate note of any idea that struck him, frequently writing his thoughts down in the middle of the night in total darkness, then deciphering the scribble with difficulty in the morning. He left his cell only for Mass and for meals, but he had frequent visitors from among the monks and from the neighboring English Seminary, "for he was good and pleasant company " (*Memorials,*

121). After a while he was forced to ask his guests to come during regular visiting hours, in order to avoid too much distraction. Some of the works he wrote at this time were *Of Refection, Of Patience, Of Restitution,* the incomplete *Autobiography,* several long treatises on mental prayer, and two treatises on the English Mission.

As time passed, Baker had more and more visitors to his cell; and he gained more and more disciples to his method of prayer. This situation led inevitably to resentment on the part of some of the superiors, who felt that their authority and prestige were being undercut. One source of trouble arose from a dispute at Douay concerning the definition of "internal obedience." It was Baker's teaching that internal obedience meant an inner submission or willingness when obeying commands to do external things. Purely internal matters, however, such as one's contemplative life or methods of prayer, should not be subjected to forceful interference. For the superior to impose rigid directions on his charges' interior life would violate "that liberty which God and the Holy Church had given them" (*Memorials,* 135).

In answer to Baker's theory and to an attempted compromise by Rudisind Barlow, the President of the Congregation, Fr. Clement Reyner, stated that "nothing but an universall and unlimited and an obedience *in omnibus* would content him. . . . He hated this mincing of obedience as with a choping knife" (*Memorials,* 137–38). Baker, who was preparing notes for a treatise explaining his position on obedience, was ordered to stop all discussion of the subject. Probably he had again been misconstrued, as at Cambray; for his argument in *Sancta Sophia* (2.2.14) is not that superiors have no authority to insist on full obedience, internal and external, but that they ought to be careful how they exercise this authority in order to avoid stifling the development of their charges. The Benedictine Rule itself puts some limitation on the authority of religious superiors, but the limit is not entirely clear.

Unfortunately, Fr. Reyner's command silencing Baker came too late, though Baker obeyed it immediately, because the president "had forgot that he resided then at Doway, being an university, and in a college where were many young and spritely divines." The discussion, naturally, became general; and this situation further aggravated relations between Baker and Reyner, in spite of Baker's obedience. It is to the credit of Fr. Rudisind Barlow, who had charge of the students, that he permitted them complete liberty of discussion, "not only among themselves, but also against their master." The controversy gradually died out "without further bloud shed or losse," but the damage to Baker had been done (*Memorials*, 136, 138).

Before, the various superiors in Douay had been glad to give their charges permission to visit Baker for advice and direction, but now some of them forbade further visits. The new confessor at Cambray also complained of Baker's influence and tried to have him moved further away from Cambray, although Baker had had almost no contact with the nuns since leaving the convent. At this time, requests came both from Cambray and from the Carmelites in Antwerp, who had seen some of his treatises, asking him to come as a spiritual adviser; but, under obedience to Fr. Reyner, Baker declined. The request from the Carmelites was a considerable compliment to him as a director and as a mystic, for this invitation came from the order of St. Teresa and St. John of the Cross, one of the great contemplative orders of the time.

IX   *The English Mission*

In January, 1636, Baker completed the *Treatise of the English Mission*, [23] which discussed the spiritual dangers that confronted Benedictine missionaries, who were necessarily separated from their monasteries and from the guidance and safety of community life. From the many years that he himself had spent outside the monastery, Baker knew how many temptations and distractions the missionaries faced; in particular, he was aware how hard it was for them to preserve and develop their interior lives. Fr. Rudisind Barlow, who had been quarreling with some of the missionaries, took Baker's treatise as an argument for ending the English Benedictine mission entirely. Barlow's annoyance at the Benedictine missionaries had some justification; for, of the nine missionaries in England in 1637, two were recalcitrant monks who refused to accept the union or obey orders. Nevertheless, Barlow was continually involving himself in disputes, such as the "new wrecking controversies" that revolved around Bishop Richard Smith. [24]

It is understandable that Baker, who hated controversies, did not like to see himself drawn into one. Disturbed by the twisting of his treatise to suit Fr. Barlow's purposes, in 1638 he wrote *An*

Introduction or Preparative to a Treatise of the English Mission, in which he pointed out that there were often faults in community life as well as on the mission. He especially criticized personal ambition and the neglect of spiritual recollection.[25] The treatise contains a portrait of a spiritually distracted and ambitious monk, said to be based on the character of Fr. Rudisind Barlow. Barlow, the most noted theologian of the congregation, had held a succession of offices: twice he had been president of the English Congregation, twice prior of St. Gregory's, and he was a professor of theology at the College of St. Vedast. Fond of refereeing disputes within the Order, he was an active and busy man with little time for interior prayer. He had earlier sent Baker to Cambray and had been on the commission that approved Baker's writings after the dispute with Fr. Hull. He had also sent Dom Peter Salvin, Baker's biographer, to see Baker for spiritual advice in 1630; and, upon Fr. Salvin's return to Douay, he had given him some of Baker's treatises to read (Salvin, 8, 14). He admired but he did not understand Baker, and he gradually grew cool toward him. Once again, it was the antagonism of the active and the contemplative.

When Baker had finished this second mission treatise, he asked Dom Barlow to come to his cell. After prostrating himself before Barlow, he gave him the treatise, which he said (and believed) he had written and dedicated to him under obedience to God. Barlow returned a few days later and thanked him, promising to mend his ways. According to Pritchard, he was apparently sincere; but he proved unwilling to give up any of his time-consuming offices and soon returned to his former activities.

Shortly afterward, Fr. Rudisind and the Prior of Douay, Fr. Joseph Frere, asked the president of the congregation for permission to discharge the monastery of a few monks, for owing to the Thirty Years' War, there was not enough income to feed everyone. In fact, the monastery was experiencing considerable difficulty at this time.[26] A few weeks later, Baker and Pritchard received letters from Fr. Reyner, ordering them to go on the English Mission. Baker was offered the choice of going to his nominal home monastery at Dieulward. This was not a happy alternative, however, since the English Congregation's report of 1637 to Spain notes that, owing to the wars which the King of France had "set on foot" in the area, only four or five of the original twenty monks remained there, "and moreover the greater part of them died of sickness caused by the misery and lack of necessaries." Fr. Reyner himself had suffered from the war: he was driven from Rintelin in Westphalia, where he had been prior, by the King of Sweden's armies. The refugee monks arrived in Douay in 1633, while the chapter was considering the dispute between Baker and Hull "like poor soldiers in a body, without habit, without anything." [27]

England was not the only place at this time where Catholic monks were experiencing difficulties, although there the difficulties were more organized. Therefore, although Fr. Reyner may have been technically correct when he ordered Baker to Dieulward or to England, the situation made this no real choice. Also, while it may have been necessary to send a few of the monks away on account of the food shortage, the choice of Baker and Pritchard is difficult to defend. Baker's health had seriously deteriorated, but his pleas of age and illness were disallowed. He was given another companion, Fr. Peter Salvin, who from the time of his visit to Baker at Cambray had been using his method of prayer.

Baker's action in writing the second treatise on the mission and presenting it to Barlow has been called a "false step" and a "grave lapse of judgement" by Justin McCann (Salvin and Cressy, xxxviii). It was hardly tactful. Nevertheless, it should be remembered that one of Baker's main ends in life was to champion the importance of prayer and the development of the interior life of the monastic. Fr. Barlow undoubtedly represented in his eyes that life of outward activity, lacking in spirituality, which he had first encountered in Padua, and which from the time of his third conversion he had devoted his life to combating. The impulse—setting aside as unprovable the possibility of divine guidance—was not a personal one; it came from a heartfelt desire to reform and spiritualize his order.

On the day of his departure for England, Baker's cell, much to the annoyance of his superiors, was crowded with visitors from the English Seminary, who had come to take leave of their friend. In fact, he was offered a place there by its president, Dr. Kellison, but refused, thinking that acceptance would bring shame on the monastery. Baker and his two disciples took a coach to Dunkirk, for he was too infirm to ride. There they were told that the English pass officer was turning back all Catholics, but they somehow got on board a ship. During the crossing, which took two days because of a calm, Baker occasionally forgot where he was, alarming his disciples by calling them "Father," and sometimes breaking out aloud in the course of his prayers. Luckily, Pritchard knew of a friendly customs officer in Dover, and they got safely ashore. All three, being priests ordained on the Continent, were technically guilty of treason, and could have been arrested as soon as they stepped ashore, then tried and executed.

Baker's patient acceptance of this trial—considering his age, his health, and the fact that to compel someone to go on the English mission was unheard of—exonerates him of any suspicion of failure to respect the idea of proper obedience to authority. Although he continually advocated spiritual freedom for those living an interior life, he considered the commands of superiors, when unpleasant, to be necessary mortifications which had to be submitted to. He did not even take advantage of his right to appeal—although all of his friends urged him to do so—because he wanted to avoid the appearance of contentiousness when only his personal comfort and safety were involved. His two major conflicts, with Hull and Barlow, were about points of spirituality that he felt obliged to defend at whatever cost to himself; but in this purely personal matter he submitted without argument.

There is a passage in Baker's first mission treatise, finished two years earlier, which is an ironic commentary on the events of 1638:

Fa: Rudisind Barlow who havinge lived and professed in Spaine, came thence as towards the mission of England about the yeare of 1611, and arrived at Doway at the time that the howse of St Gregory was in beginninge to be founded and buillt by the good Abbot of Arras; and there ever since the said father as yet remayneth fixed, and went no farther for England. I say *as yet*, because I can promise no mans not goinge and passinge to England, save mine owne whose body is so extreamly decayed, that if it intended such a thinge, it would not suffise for it but would faile by death ere it could well reach halfe the way; otherwise I could not promise never to coveit the iourney, such naturall motives may and usually do arise in men towards it. (*Memorials*, 183)

In the margin of the Ampleforth MS someone has written: "The author himselfe contrary to expectation is now gone by obedience. I pray God blisse him and be his comfort, as he hath beene a comfort to many" (*Memorials*, 183 *n*).

In London, Baker returned to his old lodgings in Gray's Inn Lane, but circumstances forced him to move. Also, at about this same time, a letter arrived from Douay which was so critical of Baker that the Benedictine Provincial in England refused to have anything to do with him. His health had worsened again, and for a while he was forced to keep to his bed. He was moved to a third lodging, then to a fourth in Holborn, where he stayed at the house of Mrs. Agnes Watson, the mother of a nun at Cambray. In the meantime, Salvin and Pritchard had been forced by their duties to leave him. Since his return to England Baker had given up all further writing, aside from a few short letters, for he had lost both the inspiration and the ability to write. During these final years, however, he may have reached a state of passive contemplation—a possibility to be further considered at the end of the next chapter.

In November, 1640, at the beginning of the Long Parliament, the pursuivants grew very active in searching out and arresting Catholics. Baker's presence with Mrs. Watson was betrayed to them, so he was again forced to move from lodging to lodging. At one time, when the pursuivants were about to break down the door of a deserted house where Baker was hiding, someone in the street called that the plague was suspected there and frightened them off. This frequent moving about, together with his age and his weak constitution, at last proved too much for him. He grew weaker and went to bed with a high fever. On the third day he took a pen and wrote: "Abstinence and Resignation, I see must be my condition, to my very expiration" (*Cressy*, 139). On the following day, August 9, 1641, at the age of sixty-five, he died. He was buried in St. Andrew's, Holborn, probably by Mrs. Watson. According to Pritchard, when Baker was on the point of death, "he wished that he might dy without anie company about him; and I think he did so" (*Memorials*, 154).

At the last, Baker had returned to London, where he had been drawn so many times before in earlier years, first by his father's ambition and then by the exigencies of his religion; it was here that he had once long ago told Dom Pritchard that he expected to die (*Memorials*, 154). It was fitting that the man who had done so much to revive the English Congregation and who tried to revitalize the tradition of English mysticism, should have died in Eng-

land. At the same time, it was tragic that his last years were spent
in virtual exile from his order because of the antagonism of a few
men who disliked him. He had made many firm friends during the
course of his life, but for following his convictions he died alone.
Nevertheless, this culmination was partly his wish, and a fitting
one to a mystical life: to be alone with God at the end.

CHAPTER 3

Baker as Mystic

NONE of Baker's ideas about spirituality or mysticism are novel or unorthodox; in fact, they were twice examined by delegation and three times approved in solemn session by the whole chapter of English Benedictines. Father Francis Hull's complaint against Baker came before the General Chapter of 1633, which appointed a delegation to examine his writings. This delegation, consisting of Fr. Leander of San Martino (Leander Jones), and, ironically, Fr. Rudisind Barlow, gave his works an unqualified approval. Some of the comments they made are printed in an appendix to the 1876 edition of *Sancta Sophia* (pp. 551–62). In 1653 Baker's doctrines were unanimously approved by another General Chapter, many of whose members knew him and his writings; and at this time Fr. Cressy was delegated to make a summary of Baker's treatises for publication. Finally, in 1657, a third General Chapter authorized the publication of *Sancta Sophia* "at the Charges of his Conuent of S. Gregories, in Doway." [1]

It is to be hoped, however, that these indications of orthodoxy will not make it appear that Baker's work is entirely derivative or uninteresting. Certain elements in it distinguish his teaching from that of other mystics. His doctrines were collectively known in his time as "Bakerism," by friends and enemies alike, although he himself tried to say that he taught nothing but ordinary Christianity. It has often been said that heresy is the result of overemphasis on one element or another of orthodoxy, to the exclusion of others. By the same token, orthodoxy itself can be given a new direction, or can become fresher and more germane, by stressing ideas which, while previously accepted, remained dormant or undeveloped.

There are a few key ideas in Baker's writings which are central to his approach to spirituality, and which at the same time characterize his thought and set it apart from that of other mystics.

While these ideas were not invented by Baker, the particular use that he makes of them and the stress that he gives them result in a significant, original contribution to mystical literature. In this study three topics that are central to his teaching and characteristic of his approach to mysticism are examined. These are his insistence on the precedence of will to understanding, and experience to learning, in contemplation and its approaches; his emphasis on inspiration and spiritual freedom; and his adherence to a *via media* of practicality in his approach to the mystical way and to asceticism. The balance of the present chapter prepares the ground for studying these points by considering Baker's writing and teaching as a whole.

It is better to trace these key ideas through the whole of Baker's writings than to approach them work by work. For one thing, Baker repeats himself, not only in the original manuscripts but even in the published works. Furthermore, Baker with a few exceptions does not appear to have reversed himself or held contradictory opinions at different times. One possible exception is his treatment of passive contemplation, which involves apparent inconsistencies that will be discussed later in this chapter; and other minor exceptions are noted as they occur. It was observed in the previous chapter that the treatises that Baker wrote at Douay differed from those of Cambray, but this difference was due to a change in audience rather than philosophy. Perhaps the uniformity in Baker's mystical writing is due in part to the circumstance that he began writing at a late age, when his views were already well matured.

I *The Mystical Tradition*

Before proceeding to a consideration of Baker's approach to mysticism, it is necessary to review briefly some of the salient conceptions of mysticism and to explain a few terms. Mysticism—as it is here treated—must be limited to the Christian and particularly to the orthodox Catholic tradition, since any broadening of scope would lead to considerable complication.

The final goal of the mystic is nothing less than God Himself. His desire is to know and to love God, not by report or by ordinary faith, but directly. By means of prayer and mortification, less and less by his own efforts, as progress is made, and more and more by God's intervention, the mystic rises above attachment to created things, to sense imagery, and even to human ideals, until he comes at last to love God for Himself alone. The final stage in the mystical way is the actual union between God and the soul, in which the soul is transformed; this state is the closest that man can come to the Beatific Vision before death.

This process of rising above the things of the senses is not to be understood as a progressive intellectual abstraction, which empties itself of the reality of objects, and thus becomes merely their imaginary common denominator, less real than any one of them. According to St. John of the Cross, those abstractions from created things that are the product of imagination or fancy are of less worth than the things themselves; and they do not help lead the soul to God:

> Imagination cannot fashion or imagine anything whatsoever beyond that which it has experienced through its exterior senses—namely, that which it has seen with the eyes, or heard with the ears, etc. At most it can only compose likenesses of those things that it has seen or heard or felt, which are of no more consequence than those which have been received by the senses aforementioned, nor are they even of as much consequence. For, although a man imagines palaces of pearls and mountains of gold, because he has seen gold and pearls, all this is in truth less than the essence of a little gold or of a single pearl, although in the imagination it be greater in quantity and in beauty. And since . . . no created things can bear any proportion to the Being of God, it follows that nothing that is imagined in their likeness can serve as a proximate means to union with Him, but, as we say, quite the contrary.[2]

It should also be kept in mind that mysticism is not considered by its practitioners to be unrealistic or theoretical: to them, it is a way of life; *the* way of life to those who are capable of it. In McCann's words, "mysticism proper—as distinguished from philosophical theory or vague feeling or literary pleasure—is a practical thing, something more than a doctrine, a life" (*Commentary*, x).

Although the individual can prepare himself for contemplation, putting himself with the help of ordinary grace—by means of retirement from activity, meditative prayer, and mortification—into a condition in which he is ready to respond to God, there is nevertheless a certain point which cannot be passed without the special intervention of God. True mystical prayer cannot be attained by the soul's unaided efforts; for, according to Poulain, "the two essential points of difference which separate the mystical state from ordinary prayer are experimental knowledge and passivity." [3] Although the soul must continually exert itself by remaining faithful to God between mystical experiences and by disposing itself for His intervention, these experiences themselves become more and more passive. The working of God in the soul, which is at first obscure and unseen, finally becomes so strong that the soul is often incapable of independent action during recollection.

Mystical writers agree that advancement in prayer must be accompanied by mortification; therefore the mystical way is sometimes called the ascetical way. While writers differ as to the propriety of voluntary self-mortifications, all agree that mortification is involved in the very nature of mysticism; for abstraction from things and from the self, necessary if the soul is to conform with God, must always be a painful and difficult process. This is not to say that the mystical life is not also a joyful one, since mystics count what they gain to be greater than what they sacrifice; but it is certainly a way full of difficulties and testings of the spirit. Great courage and perseverance are necessary, and to be a half-hearted or half-committed mystic is impossible.

Although the Catholic mystic believes that all true mysticism must have the same goal, namely God, there have been many different approaches. This variety is due partly to the difficulty of expressing in words the inherently inexpressible, so that similar experiences are described with completely different sets of imagery or terminology; partly to the fact that there actually appear to be a number of different ways which mystics have taken. According to St. John of the Cross, "God raises every soul by different paths. Scarcely shall you find one soul that in half its way agrees with that of another." [4]

Although mysticism has often been schematized, and this is necessary if one is to discuss it, one stage of the mystical way blends into another, so it is better to think of it as a continuous progression, sometimes slow and sometimes rapid, rather than as a series of steps. The image of a ladder, with each rung representing a stage on the way, is often used, but cannot be taken too literally. What Watkin says of the transition from ordinary to mystical prayer applies also to the later stages: "We have therefore no reason to expect any distinct line of demarcation between

the ordinary life of grace and mystical experience or prayer.
. . . It is true that there can be no confusion between ordinary prayer and well-marked mystical states. But it is impossible
to state clearly where ordinary prayer ends and mystical experience begins." [5]

The first step of the mystical way in the majority of cases—what
Baker calls the "ordinary" way (*Commentary,* 159)—is for the
mystic to prepare the ground by retiring from the world, by putting distractions out of mind, and by giving up all ambitions that
might interfere with the spiritual life. Usually, these preliminaries
are accomplished by entering a monastery, although Baker says
that contemplation is possible, if rare, outside the religious life
(*Sancta Sophia,* 1.3.1). Next, ordinarily, comes meditation, a kind
of mental prayer in which the individual calls up a picture of
some event of religious significance, like the Passion or the Last
Supper, trying to see it as vividly and concretely as possible. He
then employs the feelings aroused by this mental picture to direct
acts of love, thanks, or the like, toward God.

Perhaps the best-known and most influential work on the subject of meditation in Baker's time was the *Spiritual Exercises* of St.
Ignatius, but many other books on meditation appeared during
the period.[6] Meditation is not contemplation. By stressing the importance of concrete imagery, meditation is actually the direct opposite of contemplation; but, nevertheless, meditation usually pre-
cedes it. According to Baker, all mystical writers "agree in this:
that never doth God call or enable a soul to the exercise of [con-
templation] . . . without precedent exercise of meditation or
acts. . . . And therefore was it that St Bernard said that contemplation without precedent meditation was miraculous" (*Commentary,* 174).

When, by means of meditation, reading, and spiritual direction,
the soul has been prepared and the distractions of the world have
been driven out, the apprentice mystic proceeds to exclude all
sense imagery and discursive reasoning from his prayer, or even
pictures and concepts of God, and to wait lovingly on God in a
state of quietness. This state is essentially passive, but the passivity differs from that of Quietism because the soul has worked hard
to abstract itself from the world and, in a sense, continues to do so
in order to hold itself properly disposed. This state of prayer, the
threshold of contemplation, is variously called the "prayer of

faith" (de Besse), "prayer of loving attention" (St. John), "prayer
of simple committal to God or simple dwelling in the presence of
God" (St. Francis de Sales), "prayer of simplicity" (Poulain), or
"prayer of interior silence" (Baker).[7]

This catalogue of names may help to suggest what this state of
prayer is and may also show how hard it is, even at the lowest
stages, to find a terminology for mystical experience. It is in this
prayer that the individual reaches the limit obtainable by human
effort assisted by ordinary grace. Here, if He wishes, God inter-
venes in the development of the soul; and here mystical prayer
properly begins. Although some writers have put true mysticism
at a much higher stage, St. John of the Cross insists that God's
active intervention begins here, although He acts subtly and imperceptibly for a time.[8]

The first stage of contemplation, which St. John calls "loving
attention" and Baker "interior silence," resembles a descent into
obscurity and nothingness in the soul. The titles of mystical works
like *The Dark Night of the Soul*, *The Cloud of Unknowing*, or
Hid Divinity indicate its nature. Even St. Thomas Aquinas, who
attempted to rationalize theology as far as he could, writes: "As
Dionysius says (*Ep. i, ad Caium. Monach.*), *if anyone seeing
God, understood what he saw, he saw not God Himself, but something belonging to God.*" [9] Because God is transcendent, there is
no proportion at all between Him and creation. The mystic, who
must strip away all ways of looking at God that derive from sense
experience, is thus left with nothing; but this nothing is filled with
an increasing sense of the presence of God in the soul. Therefore,
mystics speak often in terms of a simultaneous presence of darkness and light.

A familiar example of the mystical process is found in the experience of St. Augustine. A major theme of the *Confessions* is his
progress from thinking of divinity as something material to the
realization that God is a pure spirit to be sought within the soul.
In a passage that describes this mystical experience, St. Augustine
comments on the paradox that God is both everything and nothing:

And Thou didst beat back the weakness of my sight, streaming forth
Thy beams of light upon me most strongly, and I trembled with love
and awe: and I perceived myself to be far off from Thee, in the region

of unlikeness, as if I heard this Thy voice from on high: "I am the food of grown men; grow, and thou shalt feed upon Me; nor shalt thou convert Me, like the food of thy flesh into thee, but thou shalt be converted into Me." And I learned, that Thou for iniquity chastenest man, and Thou madest my soul to consume away like a spider. And I said, "Is truth therefore nothing because it is not diffused through space finite or infinite?" And Thou criedst to me from afar: "Yet verily, I AM that I AM." And I heard, as the heart heareth, nor had I room to doubt, and I should sooner doubt that I live than that Truth is not.[10]

The phrase "region of unlikeness" stresses God's transcendence from creation. God has no dimensions, and in physical terms is nothing. At the same time, He is existence itself: " 'I AM that I AM.' " St. Augustine does not pretend to understand the mystery, but at the same time he is surer of God's existence than of his own. Thus the mystical experience involves both a realization of ignorance and a new confidence and feeling of surety.

In his road upward, the mystic must undergo certain purgations of his soul, which St. John of the Cross calls "the four nights." These are, in order, the active night of sense, the active night of spirit, the passive night of sense, and the passive night of spirit. The nights of sense consist of mortification and withdrawal of the desires from all created things. The nights of the spirit, in part at least, involve rejection of all spiritual goods and virtues less than God himself. According to Watkin, "The Active Nights constitute the purgation accomplished by the soul's own will, of course with the assistance of Divine grace. The two Passive Nights constitute the deeper purgation effected in the soul by the mystical experience itself. . . . The Passive, unlike the Active, Nights are . . . themselves constituent parts of that union." [11]

After the prayer of loving attention, which is preceded and accompanied by the active nights, come the higher stages of the contemplative way. Since Baker's teachings are mainly concerned with the earlier phases, these states may be briefly summarized. Watkin gives five divisions, basing his terminology on the writings of St. Teresa and St. John: the passive night of sense, quiet, ecstasy, the passive night of spirit; and finally the spiritual betrothal and mystical marriage.[12] As we shall see, Baker probably did not reach any of these stages of prayer before his return to England in 1638; and, while there are grounds for believing that he may have reached them in the last few years of his life, he had then stopped writing. As a result, his teachings are not concerned with the heights of contemplation, except briefly and at second hand.

II *The Call to Contemplation*

From the time that Baker entered the monastery of St. Justina's in Padua, if not before, he had been attracted to the interior life, drawn to the contemplative way by something in his nature. If at first it may seem surprising or even reprehensible that he twice fell away from this course that he was so particularly fitted for (especially the second time, after he had gotten as far as he had), we should remember that the circumstances were not favorable. It is, in fact, surprising that he ever got as far as he did without real guidance and with only a vague understanding of what he was seeking. Even St. Teresa experienced her decisive conversion to contemplation fully twenty years after first entering a convent; and Balthazar Alvarez, the Jesuit whose life Baker thought resembled his own, spent sixteen years in fruitless efforts to meditate before discovering the prayer of loving attention.[13]

Throughout Baker's *Inner Life of Dame Gertrude More*, he stresses the necessity of a strong "propension," or "propensity," toward God in anyone who would become a mystic. This propensity, which is found in the superior will, is defined as a strong, steady, often submerged desire to seek God directly by means of prayer and to overcome all obstacles which intervene. Without this gift, a natural talent that cannot normally be acquired, no one would have the perseverance to continue very long in the contemplative way. It cannot be doubted that Baker came to hold this view (which is orthodox, since not everyone is fitted for contemplation) through self-examination. His own propensity to contemplation is clearly evident in his life: not only in his efforts, finally successful, to become a mystic but even more clearly in the discontent and restlessness which he felt whenever he abandoned prayer. He was motivated by an inner urge, and books served only to clarify a desire which he already felt.

In the course of his conversions and relapses, Baker came to believe that it was supremely important for anyone called to the contemplative life to respond to that call. In the *Inner Life of Dame Gertrude More* he writes: "For a soul capable of an interior life this should be all in all. Woe, woe—yea, a thousand times woe!—to the soul that is frightened by threats, overcome by temptations, cast by fear into perplexities, which render her unfit to hear or follow what God speaks to her, and discouraged from pursuing prayer, which may be called omnipotent, so powerful is it with God!" (205).

The importance of prayer is even greater in the case of those who have entered the religious orders. Writing, we may assume, from his own former experience and also from the practical insight gained by his work with Dame Gertrude and the other nuns, he says that those who enter a religious order but do not live a life of interior prayer are worse off than anyone. For worldly people at least enjoy worldly pleasures, but a religious without the interior life is cut off both from the world and from God, and left with nothing (*Commentary,* 167). Elsewhere, Baker insists on "the practice of pure contemplative prayer, without which a religious state would be no better than a mere outward occupation or trade." [14]

Baker thought that life under the Benedictine Rule could be happy and contented only if all those capable of it put themselves into the mystical way and progressed as far along it as God enabled them. Even a small number of contemplatives would act as a leaven to the rest and would by their examples lead others into the way, as, in fact, did Baker himself: "A few such secret and unknown servants of God are the *chariots and horsemen,* the strength and bulwarks of the kingdoms and churches where they live" (*Confessions,* 49). This call to contemplation was the positive message of Baker's second mission treatise, which resulted in his being sent to England in 1638.

It had long been the opinion of orthodox Catholic writers that the contemplative life was superior to the active. The primary text for this teaching is Christ's rebuke of Martha (Luke, 10:38–42), in which Martha is interpreted to represent the active life and Mary the contemplative. Concerning contemplation, St. Thomas says: "The contemplative life is simply more excellent than the active." One reason he gives is that "The active life ends with this world, but the contemplative life begins here, to be perfected in our heavenly home." [15]

III   *The First Stages*

According to Baker, those who decide to become contemplatives, or rather feel themselves called to it, must normally first prepare themselves by retirement from activity, mortification, and non-mystical prayer. There are four kinds of prayer which Baker believed might be used to lead the soul to contemplation: vocal prayer, meditation, sensible affections, and immediate acts. The prayers used depend on the nature of the person, and are to be treated as means to an end, which is contemplation. Baker writes: "When the soul has attained to contemplation, it makes not the least difference as to which of the four paths she has travelled—all ways meet in contemplation, and contemplation is alike for all, the only difference being that some souls rise higher out of their sensible natures than others" (*Inner Life,* 71).

In the *Inner Life of Dame Gertrude More,* the four kinds of prayer are put more or less on a level with one another, at least in comparison with mystical prayer. In *Sancta Sophia,* greater precedence is given to immediate acts of the will, since the treatise on prayer is divided into three sections: meditation, forced acts, and contemplation. This arrangement has led to charges that Baker put too much emphasis on prayer of the will, and even that he confused this kind of prayer with contemplation itself.[16] The charge is unfounded, though it is true that Baker does not always make the line of separation as clear as he might. It is impossible, however, to qualify every statement every time it is made, especially in a subject as complicated as mysticism; indeed, Baker's style is too clogged by qualifications.

Vocal prayer is the most elementary of the stages which lead into the mystical way. By vocal prayer, Baker means spoken prayer accompanied by inward attention, since "vocal prayer, as distinguished from . . . mental, is indeed no prayer at all" (*Sancta Sophia,* 3.1.1.9). According to Baker, vocal prayer was at one time used exclusively to lead to contemplation: "In ancient times many holy souls did attain to perfect contemplation by the mere use of vocal prayer; the which likewise would have the same effect upon us if we would or could imitate them both in such wonderful solitude or abstraction, rigorous abstinences, and incredible assiduity in praying" (*Sancta Sophia,* 3.1.2.2). Like many other seventeenth-century writers, Baker believed that the men of his time were of lesser stature and potential than those of an earlier age.[17] The use of vocal prayer, for this reason, would (he thought) lead directly to contemplation only in unusual cases.

The first step toward contemplation for most, in Baker's view, is the prayer of meditation. His definition of meditation in *Sancta Sophia,* concisely and carefully phrased, is worth giving in full:

Meditation is such an internal prayer in which a devout soul doth, in the first place, take in hand the consideration of some particular mystery of faith, to the end that, by a serious and exact search into the several points and circumstances in it with the understanding or imagination, she may extract motives of good affections to God, and consequently produce suitable affections in virtue of the said motives as long as such virtue will last. (3.2.2.2)

Most people should begin their meditation in the "purgative way," considering such topics as sin, death, or judgment; but the scrupulous or fearful should omit this step. A familiar example of this kind of meditation is Donne's sonnet, "What if this Present were the World's Last Night?" When these meditations have taken effect, producing sorrow for sin and desire for reconciliation, the beginner should pass on to the "illuminative way," that is, to such topics as incidents in the life of Christ "which are apt to beget and increase humility, patience, and other virtues in her" (*Sancta Sophia,* 3.2.3.11). These meditations should be made at set times, preferably for an hour in the morning and an hour in the evening, and be prepared for by reading devotional books.

As the purpose of meditation is "to move the will to good affections," the individual should avoid making meditation "a study and speculation [rather] than an exercise of the spirit" (*Sancta Sophia,* 3.2.3.20). The idea is, therefore, to try to decrease the time spent in elaborating the incident meditated on, by dwelling longer and longer on the affections of the will which it arouses. As the soul is drawn toward God, it will need less and less material to motivate it and will be able to prolong its acts of the will. The number of topics made use of during the hour of meditation will decrease until only a few or even one are necessary.

Some people, unfortunately, for one reason or another are incapable of meditation. Women, in particular, were thought to be more inclined to love and to direct acts of the will than to complicated intellection. (Compare Milton's differentiation of Adam and Eve in *Paradise Lost,* IV.295–99.) One alternative to meditation as a preparation for the mystical way is the prayer of sensible affections. This prayer is appropriate for people who are not aroused by discursive thoughts, or who are unable to frame suitable pictures with their imaginations, but who have a strong natural tendency to be affectionate: "Such tender souls as these, having withal a natural good propension to seek God in their interior, can easily exercise their affections to God in and by their corporal nature, without troubling themselves with seeking reasons and motives for it; yea, in a short time they come to have a kind of disgust in inventing or considering motives represented by the understanding" (*Sancta Sophia*, 3.3.1.7).

Instead of fruitlessly trying to meditate in contradiction to their very natures, such people should use the prayer of sensible affection, making use of their natural passions but gradually purifying and elevating them: "The principal care that such souls ought to have is, to endeavor to raise this their love out of sensitive nature to the superior spiritual will, by whose operations alone the soul is truly perfected" (*Sancta Sophia*, 3.3.1.9). The prayer of sensible affection should undergo a gradual transformation into forced acts of the will.

IV   "*The Prayer of Acts*"

The majority probably start with meditations. If they continue in them, their acts of will and their affections toward God are strengthened and are produced with less and less preparatory motivation. Eventually, meditation turns into the prayer of forced acts, otherwise called "acts of the will," "immediate acts," or simply "the prayer of acts." In this form of prayer the act of directing the will toward God, which was the last part of meditation, predominates. At first, it may keep some of the characteristics of meditation, since the transition is gradual. Baker writes in *Sancta Sophia:*

In forced immediate acts of the will, especially at the beginning, there is some degree of meditation, which is the thinking on the object, and thereupon internally producing the act or affection itself, and quietly continuing and resting in it till all the virtue of it be spent. There is, likewise, always some use of images; and in the beginning these images are more gross, but afterwards, by practice, they grow more pure, and all manner of discourse ceaseth; yea, the soul will begin to reject all distinct images, and apprehend God without any particular representation, only by that obscure notion which faith informs us of His totality and incomprehensibility; and this only is truth, whereas all distinct images are but imperfect shadows of truth. (3.3.1.15)

The prayer of sensible affection, by the gradual elevation of the soul from the senses and the emotions to the superior will, also leads into the prayer of forced acts by a different way. Some people are fitted neither for meditation nor for the prayer of sensible affections; they must start directly with acts of the will. Baker, who seems to have been one of these, was never able to meditate profitably for very long. He evidently stumbled on the prayer of acts at Cook Hill, although he left off because of his lack of guidance. This inability to meditate may also account for the lack of colorful imagery in most of his writing; those images he uses are derived from his reading rather than from his imagination. Although contemplation itself is imageless, it does not necessarily lead to an inability in the contemplative to use imagery in his writing, as we can see in St. John of the Cross. In fact, the very opposite is often the case.

The names "forced acts" and "acts of the will" suggest a certain degree of violence in the soul. Although the terms are useful to describe some aspects of this kind of prayer, they fail to be wholly satisfactory. Baker writes in *Sancta Sophia:* "The less impetuous that the operations of the will are in this exercise of *Immediate Acts,* and the more still, quiet, peaceable, and profound that they are (so there be no wilful negligence), the more effectual and profitable are they, and the more efficacious to still passions, as also to compose and settle the imagination" (3.3.1.18). As the soul progresses in the prayer of immediate acts, the necessity for any admixture of meditation disappears, and the soul relies less and less on imagery to produce or to accompany its acts of will. The understanding is not much used, nor discursive reasoning, and periods of dryness may be experienced, in which both the understanding and the emotions are unsatisfied. This dryness must be treated as a necessary mortification, and the soul must persist in spite of all discouragements. This is one of the crucial stages in the contemplative way, since the use of natural reason has been for the most part abandoned; but the soul has not yet entered into real contemplative prayer. Great perseverance is needed, and the encouragement of a spiritual director is almost a necessity.

Between the section on acts of the will and the section on contemplation in *Sancta Sophia,* Cressy inserts a short chapter on the prayer of interior silence, which is usually considered by mystics to be the form of prayer which is at the threshold of true contemplation. Baker bases his exposition of it on the *Life of the Spirit Approved,* by Antonio de Rojas. Like Bennett Canfield's book, *The Rule of Perfection,* Rojas's work was placed on the Index because it tended toward Quietism, but there is no reflection of this tendency in Baker's adaption. To use this form of prayer, Baker writes, the soul must quit all direct acts or affections:

All that remains for her then to do is, with all humility and love, to continue in His presence in the quality of a petitioner, but such an one as makes no special direct requests, but contents herself to appear before Him with all her wants and necessities, best, and indeed only, known to Him, who therefore needs not her information; so that she with a silent attention regards God only, rejecting all manner of images of all objects whatsoever, and with the will she frames no particular request nor any express acts towards God, but remains in an entire silence both of tongue and thoughts. (3.3.7.5)

Baker does not clearly explain the place that this prayer of interior silence has in the path to contemplation. According to Gerard Sitwell, he "seems to regard it as an alternative to the prayer of forced acts rather than as a complement to it, which at times the soul can hardly avoid, and which it is not desirable it should avoid." [18] But there is nothing in the chapter to indicate that Baker is presenting it as an alternative prayer; indeed, it is not included among the four kinds of preparatory prayer mentioned in *The Inner Life,* nor does Dom Peter Salvin include it in his summary of Baker's method. Baker seems to have been uncertain where the prayer of interior silence could be fitted into his scheme, and Cressy may have placed it where it is in *Sancta Sophia* because he knew from other sources that it belonged immediately before contemplation.

In a number of places, however, Baker implies that the soul proceeds directly from the prayer of acts to the prayer of aspirations, which (according to his nomenclature) is the lowest stage of true contemplation. No distinct mention is made of the prayer of interior silence anywhere in *Sancta Sophia* except in the one chapter at the end of the section on forced acts. A reasonable conclusion is that Baker did not think of the prayer of interior silence as coming between the prayer of acts and proper aspirations. One passage in *Sancta Sophia* supports this view:

In passing from the exercise of acts to Aspirations there is, as to the manner of the cessation of forced acts, great variety in souls; for some will have their morning recollections to be suddenly and entirely changed from forced acts to Aspirations, and also the ability for a longer continuance increased; whereas, the evening recollections will be little altered. In other souls (and this is most ordinary), their exercising of acts will grow by degrees more and more aspirative, and this will happen sometimes in the beginning, sometimes in the middle, and sometimes in the conclusion of their recollections. And thus they in their recollections will get more and more ground upon acts, diminishing both the frequency and constraint or difficulty of them, and increasing Aspirations, till in progress they become wholly aspirative. (3.4.2.11)

This passage clearly states the possibility of proceeding from acts to aspirations without the intervention of an intermediate form of prayer, and it is not explicitly contradicted anywhere in the chapter on prayer of interior silence. It appears, therefore, that Baker does not consider the prayer of interior silence to be a separate stage in the soul's development but tacitly includes it in the prayer of acts. It was noted above that he did not mean to suggest violent movements within the soul when he talked about acts of will; for he says that "the more still, quiet, peaceable, and profound that they are (so there be no wilful negligence), the more effectual and profitable are they." This kind of "forced acts" could easily culminate in the prayer of loving attention, which involves a certain use of the will in disposing the soul to receive God's guidance.[19] The quoted passage may, then, refer to what is in reality prayer of interior silence; and the admonition to avoid "wilful negligence" may be a warning against the dangers of Quietism. Baker, because of opposition to his teachings about forced acts, sometimes overstresses the importance of will; but, when acts of will are "quiet, peaceable, and profound," they become nearly indistinguishable from the state in which the soul is held in passivity.

V *Contemplative Prayer*

The prayer of aspirations is the first stage of true mystical prayer, for the preceding exercises have all been intended to prepare the soul for contemplation. At this point, however, the individual can go no further by his own efforts; he must continue in the prayer of forced acts until he is brought forward by God Himself. In Baker's words, "let her continue quietly her exercises, and not cease till God force her to cease them." [20] Above all, the soul must not expect or desire visions or other extraordinary manifestations; it must wait patiently.

In the *Commentary,* Baker notes that God calls a few souls in an "extraordinary" way; two examples are St. Catherine of Siena and St. Teresa. Most contemplatives, however, must prepare themselves laboriously, rising through the stages of prayer discussed above before they can expect God's intervention: "Those extraordinary saints God prevented with his graces and favours; but we must after a manner prevent him by our industries, together with his grace" (160–61). For this reason, Baker spends so much time discussing the preliminaries of the mystical way, and so little time on true mysticism. In "Of Finding God Within Our Soul," he writes that, even in the preparatory stages, God's grace is more responsible for progress than the soul's industry; in contemplation itself, ordinary grace must be superseded by a special kind of grace. In spite of this necessity, however, God "never faileth to do it, to a soul well disposed for it, which must be by a long use of prayer, seriously prosecuted, with competent abstraction of life and other mortifications." [21]

Aspirations resemble acts of the will, with these two chief differences: they are more spiritual and abstracted from the use of imagery, and they are produced by the hidden action of God in the soul, not by the soul's own initiative. Baker is not, however, totally consistent in his use of the term "aspirations"; he seems to include under it prayers which make some use of imagery and involve the active exercise of the will. The difficulty results because acts of will and proper aspirations blend into one another. In *Sancta Sophia* (3.4.2.9), one passage suggests that imperfect aspirations may sometimes be intermixed with forced acts. In the *Commentary on the Cloud,* Baker describes the prayer of aspirations as a state in which the soul "bluntly or blindly heave[s] itself up towards God, apprehended only according to the general notion of faith, and so do[es] apply and unite itself unto him, without any other aspect of him, or any such joyous regard of him, as they do imagine who are acquainted only with the exercises of sense and with sensible love" (156). The natural understanding, which can work only in terms of the imagery supplied by the senses, is left behind; and the soul enters the "dark cloud of un-knowing."

The best exposition of the manner in which God acts in the soul in this kind of prayer is also found in the *Commentary on the Cloud:*

> All those several kinds and varieties of aspirations and elevations that are comprised in the work treated of in the *Cloud* do agree in this: that they proceed not merely from the man's own head, will, or election, but from the divine interior motion, intimation, and instruction, as before I have told you. It is true that the man is the agent in it; but he doth it by motion from God, who moveth his will to do it and teacheth him how to do it: in some sort as a writing master doth move and guide the hand of his young scholar when he teacheth him to write. And there-fore, in such a case, there is a double call from God. The first call is that God inciteth, moveth, and enableth the soul, without any discourse or motive of reason for it, to break forth immediately into such aspira-tions or elevations. The second call is for the manner: which is that God teacheth the soul what kind of aspirations she is to use, and in what manner to exercise them. Whereas they who are in meditation or acts do make their own choice what kind and in what manner they are to use their meditation, or to come forth with their acts. And commonly they have to search and do a little study for the matter and manner of their meditation or acts.[22] (173–74)

As in the case of his descriptions of acts of the will, Baker's lan-guage gives an impression of greater activity and movement in the soul than he really means. Just as prayer of the will can lead into prayer of interior silence, however, so prayer of aspirations can gradually and imperceptibly lead into prayer of union. An-other passage in the *Commentary* discusses this mingling of aspi-ration and union:

> The aspirations of which we have spoken are an exercise by which we immediately aspire to a perfect union with God. In the aspirations themselves there is much good love and a kind of union; but there is not in them perfect love or perfect union. The aspirations are a certain greedy longing or thirsting after God out of love; but when the soul is come to be united to him, then do they cease: she being come to enjoy and possess that Good which by her aspirations she aspired and tended unto. But such union ceasing—for it doth not always last—she re-neweth her aspirations, by them aspiring to a new union. (166)

After the prayer of aspirations, Baker places a further stage which he calls "elevation of the will" or simply "elevation." He does not, however, draw a distinct line between these two kinds of prayer: "I make no difference between aspiration and elevation, but that elevation doth signify a greater subtlety or spirituality, and a nearer approachment to a union than doth aspiration (*Commentary*, 167).

Beyond elevation of the will comes what Baker calls "the state of active union," "perfect active union," or "infused active union." He uses the term "active" differently from most mystical writers, for Baker clearly refers to the very highest reaches of mystical prayer, while most writers reserve it to describe lower states, calling the highest "passive." Baker, however, with one possible exception, uses the term "passive" only when he refers to short-lived, temporary actions of God upon the soul. Continuous union or continuing experience of a particular level of prayer during recollection he calls "active union" or "active contemplation." He usually differentiates the higher forms of contemplation from the lower by the term "perfect," instead of "passive."

A short essay of Baker's called "Of that Mystic Saying 'Nothing and Nothing Make Nothing' " probably gives the clearest indication of what Baker means by the state of active union. Cressy used this essay for the chapter on union in *Sancta Sophia*, but it loses in the paraphrase. An extract from the original essay best presents Baker's doctrine:

For when the soul hath cast out of her understanding all naturall images and apprehensions, and out of her will all loves and affections to creatures, then is she become, as to all naturall things, as if she were nothing: being free, naked, and clean from them all, as if she were indeed nothing. . . . And indeed, in such perfect union between God and a soul, she hath no imaginary apprehension either of herselfe or of God; but being—as truely they are—meerly spirits, they remain in nothing, which yet may be termed a totality. And by this you may conceive what an active mystick union is. For it is caused by an application of the soul—being for the time ridd of all images—to God, apprehended according to faith, without any image and above all images.[23]

Elsewhere, in *The Inner Life*, Baker pictures the state of active union in one of the most striking images in his writings. The passage gives us a good idea of what contemplative prayer may have felt like to him:

Thus the Divinity is the infinite, profound centre or resting-place of man's soul, to whom all other things, especially sensible things, are narrow and unsuitable.

The Divinity, moreover, is the proper, vast element, wherein the soul should find life, and an infinite life. But when out of this element, the soul is like a whale that has been stranded in a brook: the great creature has not space enough to swim or plunge in its waters. Hence it ever desires the ocean, which, for its depth and wideness, is capable of containing it and millions of others. Here these huge creatures find no bottom, but can swim in all fullness, and enjoy security from all danger; for here they are in their element and, as it were, in their own kingdom. Thus does the contemplative soul, in virtue of her propensity, ever aspire to her centre and proper element, the simple Divinity. She thirsts after the spaciousness and infinity of God, wherein alone she can have her fill and be secure from all perils. (164–65)

The ultimate goal of the contemplative is union of the soul with God. Because of inherent weaknesses in human nature that can only be corrected after death, this union appears to annihilate the personality and the individuality of the soul: while it is in such intimate contact with God, it is unable to act, think, or even be aware of its own existence. In the Beatific Vision, the soul enjoys an even closer union with God while at the same time preserving its individuality and freedom; but this combination does not seem possible to the mystic in life: "There will be so immediate and straight an union, that in the union" the soul "shall not discern herself from God; but it will seem unto her that God and she are but one and the selfsame thing without any distinction, division or separation between them. And it will seem unto her for the time, that she is turned to be God and to have lost her being of a creature." [24]

The complete "annihilation" of self, as far as "self" means something not at one with the will of God, is the final result of such union; but the personality, the individuality, and the freedom are not annihilated—in accordance with the principle that the highest degree of freedom and the greatest degree of participation in reality can only be in conformity with God, who is Himself the principle of existence (*Sancta Sophia*, 3.4.6.9). Inevitably, there is a paradox, since Christianity has traditionally been unwilling to give up either the ultimate dependence of all creation on God or the freedom of the human will.

VI Baker and "Passive" Contemplation

In the course of the soul's progress toward perfect active union with God, it may experience one or more passive unions. Baker's picture of passive contemplation is derived from his own experience at the culmination of his second conversion at Cook Hill, when, for a period of less than a quarter of an hour, he experienced a state of what he called "passive contemplation." This experience, he wrote, changed his entire life, confirmed his faith, and made many of his beliefs clear for the first time. It seems to have been what is ordinarily known as an intellectual vision.[25]

A passage in the *Commentary on the Cloud* shows clearly what Baker usually means by passive contemplation:

A man in time, by the foresaid exercise of aspirations . . . attaineth to this abstraction. But commonly, about the middle of the way, God visiteth the soul with a passive exercise, and thereby doth wonderfully hasten the soul in her way to perfect abstraction. I would compare it to a journey of a thousand miles, that a weak-bodied man had to make on foot; and as if, when he had with much pain and difficulty gone a hundred of those miles, God by his omnipotent power should thereupon carry him and place him in one instant at the end of nine hundred of those miles. . . . Even so God, by his passive contemplation, which is not usually one-quarter of an hour's work, doth carry a soul further towards perfect abstraction than she with ordinary grace could have reached unto in ten or a dozen years with her own active exercise. (179–80)

An incidental point which this passage brings out is Baker's use of the word "exercise." Dom Gerard Sitwell criticizes him for his use of the word: "It is indeed a weakness of Baker that he tends always to regard prayer as an exercise to produce contemplation." Professor Knowles makes much the same point.[26] The word, as it occurs at the end of this passage, is open to this interpretation, and it is true that prayer that is literally an exercise of the individual initiative is not contemplative. The word also occurs, however, near the beginning of the passage in a totally different context: "God visiteth the soul with a passive exercise." It is clear from this sentence that Baker uses the word broadly, as something which is passively suffered or experienced as well as actively done. It is difficult to find unambiguous terms in discussing mystical experiences, so one must avoid jumping to conclusions about the meaning of a term or image.

At the end of his life, Baker may have had cause to change his opinions about the nature of passive contemplation. It is difficult to guess what stage his own prayer had reached at any particular time, especially since he felt that it was harmful for a mystic to talk much about his own experiences, even with his director, unless under obedience. Nevertheless his peculiar use of the term "passive" is an indication that, before 1638, he could not have reached the later stages of contemplation, in which, if the experiences of St. Teresa and St. John are typical, the action of God in the soul is too overt to be misinterpreted.[27]

In addition, certain passages in Baker's writings are in direct contradiction to what mystics have usually taught about the higher stages of prayer. In the *Commentary on the Cloud,* Baker writes: "And that enablement for future elevations is the fruit or good effect of such passive exercise. For if it had not such effect or fruit, the same passive exercise were little profitable to our soul. For our merit consisteth upon our own acts (though with the assistance of God's grace), and not in the acts or doings wherein God is the principal agent, or only doer, and we but the patient" (162). However true this may be of the active life, advancement in contemplation is usually considered to be by God's agency, although it may at first be hidden.

After Baker's return to England in 1638, he stopped writing because he no longer felt an inner call to set his ideas on paper—perhaps because he had now fulfilled his mission to others. We have, however, one brief, indirect indication of the state of his prayer shortly before his death. The following passage from Pritchard's biography has usually been taken to mean that, before his death, he had reached a continuing state of passive contemplation in the usual sense of the term. Pritchard's wording appears to be specific enough to leave little doubt in the matter:

I understood also by another letter, that he had given over all correspondence with Cambray, or anie other place or person. And because

those Dames were desirous to know something of him, among other
things which he would have me signifie to them, he bad me let them
know "that he was now *totus in passionibus,* all in suffering"; and,
"that one dram of suffering was worth more then an hundred pounds
of doing." And I remember, I wrote so to Cambray. But yet I was very
desirous to know of him, what he meant by being *totus in passionibus;*
for I knew he did not suffer by any persecution, nor wants, etc., having
so good a nurse; and yet on the other side, I wonderd if his praier or
contemplation were wholly passive. But by another letter from him,
I was confirmed in the truth of this latter. And indeed, if things be
well considered, he was well prepared, and (as I may say) ripened,
for such a state. He had near twenty years constantly and seriously
practiced mentall praier; he had bin soundly proved through the fire of
manyfold tribulations; and now being placed with this Sunamite, he
did enjoy all rest and peace: which peace both interior and exterior,
mystick authors do require, for this highest contemplation. And so, you
see, *Dominus benedixit novissimis huius Job, magis quam principio.*
(*Memorials,* 152)

That Baker did not fully understand the meaning of passive contemplation until he had finished his writing and gone on
to experience it personally does not mean, however, that his teachings are seriously vitiated. What he says about the higher states of
contemplation, with the exception of a few minor questionable
passages, is consistent with the teachings of the great mystics.
Furthermore, he never claimed to be a guide to the higher states:
they are outlined in a brief summary at the end of *Sancta Sophia*
in order to give beginners some idea of what they are aiming at;
but it was his belief that, when the soul entered the true contemplative way, it would thenceforward receive its guidance directly
from God and no longer need external guidance. This doctrine is
further examined in Chapter 5, which is concerned with Baker's
treatment of inspiration.

CHAPTER 4

Reason and Will

I *Faculty Psychology*

FROM the Classical period through the Renaissance, the dominant approach to human behavior was what is called "faculty psychology." With its roots in Aristotle and Plato, the theory was developed by St. Augustine and others and codified by the scholastic theologians. According to St. Augustine, the human soul had three higher faculties: understanding, memory, and will. Others mentioned two faculties: reason and will. These classifications persisted, with shifts in emphasis and nomenclature, well into the seventeenth century. Sir Thomas Browne, for example, wrote: "there is in our soule a kind of Triumvirate, or Triple government of three competitors," which are "affection, faith, and reason." [1] Here understanding is divided into two component but contrasting parts, faith and reason, while memory is omitted. Robert Burton, also omitting memory, declared that there were two powers in the soul, understanding and will.[2] Other variations can be found on the standard theory, but only a few of the more drastic innovators, like Thomas Hobbes, thought in very different terms.

Since Baker's approach to contemplative psychology and to the methodology of prayer involves the tacit assumption on his part of many of the theories of faculty psychology, it is helpful to review this tradition before proceeding to further analysis of his writings. Indeed, Fr. Cressy intended to include an appendix on this subject in *Sancta Sophia* for the use of the "unlearned," but lack of space forced him to omit it.[3] Although Baker—because a convert and because of the irregularities forced on the English Benedictines by exile—had no formal theological training, he seems to have absorbed the main conceptions of scholastic psychology. Some of these concepts had been retained by Protestant England, and might have been learned in school. They were part of the intellectual background of the time, changing only slowly in spite of the movement of sects or even the large-scale revolutions of religion. Others, such as the theory of the center or ground of the soul, he may have derived from his mystical reading. Although he read chiefly devotional and mystical literature, he shows at least some acquaintance with St. Thomas; and his background in scholastic psychology, if irregular, appears wide and thorough.

According to most scholastic psychologists, the human mind is at birth a *tabula rasa*.[4] Information, except in unusual or miraculous circumstances, is received only through the five senses, which present their messages to the mind by means of the imagination, a power that is understood in its literal meaning of image-making, or of presenting pictures of things to the higher powers. Imagination is also called phantasy, fantasy, or fancy; and the scholastic and early seventeenth-century usages should not be confused with the subsequent development of these terms. The units handled by the imagination and manipulated by the reasoning powers were called images or phantasms; when Baker uses the word "image," he intends it in this technical sense.

St. Augustine, and some of the later Christian Platonists, believed that man's soul might have certain elemental concepts or abstractions inherent in it from birth: buried memories of prelapsarian happiness, or inborn understanding of conceptions like justice or truth, reflections of the eternal forms; but later Scholastic philosophy dismissed this possibility, at least in this guise. According to St. Thomas, all information is received through the senses; but it is shaped and understood by the "active intellect," a doctrine that has some similarity to the theory of innate ideas, though the Thomistic intellect is a power or characteristic of the mind rather than a collection of ideas or pieces of information.[5]

Within the mind, the memory has the task of storing the sense impressions brought to it by the imagination and of delivering the pertinent images to be used when needed. Imagination also presents some of these impressions directly to the reason, which has the power to manipulate them; judgment supplies the light to choose between them or establish relative values; the whole power of rational thought is called the faculty of understanding. Will translates knowledge into action, whether purely physical, or interior (as in choosing what to think about); in other words, man's will is the power or ability to make choices. The soul is also influenced by the appetites, sensual and intellectual, irascible and concupiscible, which pull it in various directions and which should rightly be subordinated to the dictates of reason and the higher will.[6]

All these powers and functions in man have been corrupted, weakened, or perverted since the time of the fall: the understanding is weak and easily misled; the will is tainted by selfishness and pride; memory is erratic and sometimes mistaken; the appetites lead men after subordinate goods and cause them to forsake the highest good; the senses and the imagination draw the soul after evil things and are vulnerable to the suggestions of the devil. This pessimistic view was qualified by faith in man or in God, but it colored in varying degrees all theories of psychology in the main tradition of Western thought, from St. Augustine (and earlier) to the seventeenth century. The topic is so large that it can receive only passing mention, but the concept of original sin must be kept constantly in mind when discussing faculty psychology.

There is a hierarchy among the elements in man, a microcosmic analogy to the hierarchy of the universe. St. Thomas distinguishes three souls in man based on distinctions made by Aristotle: vegetable, sensitive, and rational. This series is an ascending ladder from the purely physical to the spiritual.[7] Similarly, the senses are low on the scale; imagination, higher; and understanding, higher still. The three faculties—understanding, memory, and will—are in the highest or intellectual soul; and, according to St. Augustine, they are analogous to the Trinity: memory corresponds to the Father; understanding, to the Son or divine Logos; and will, to the Holy Spirit, the divine embodiment of love. Like the Trinity, these three faculties are parts of a single, essentially undivided unity, all stemming from the center or ground of the soul, occasionally called by mystics the *scintilla synderesis* or divine spark.

Baker sometimes calls this center the "point" or "fund" of the spirit, depending on whether he is thinking in terms of mounting higher or of plunging deeper into the inner self; in the *Commentary*, he calls it "the height or top of the spirit . . . above the powers [the faculties] of it." [8] While everyone was in agreement as to the essential unity of the soul, however, few but mystics accepted the conception of a point of the spirit above the faculties. The tendency of many philosophers was to put one faculty or another at the top: to say that man was essentially will, or a reasoning being. Baker, however, much as he speaks of the will, clearly subscribed to the theory that there was a unifying point above the faculties.

After St. Augustine, the tendency was to stress the importance of two of the faculties, and to pay only lip-service to memory. Browne and Burton dropped memory entirely from their classifications. Only St. Augustine's influential enthusiasm for the miraculous powers of memory[9] and the neat analogy of his three faculties to the Trinity prevented their reduction altogether to two—to what Watkin calls the "cognitive" and the "conative" faculties.[10] Memory was particularly important to St. Augustine because he speculated that it might be the seat of those hidden reminiscences of God and of happiness that the soul, in Platonic fashion, brought with it into the world.[11] But, with the victory of Aristotelianism, memory could no longer have this function and consequently became less important. As Louis Martz has recently shown, this Neoplatonic theory of memory was widely revived in the literature of the seventeenth century,[12] but Baker follows Aristotle and St. Thomas on this point.

In Baker's published writings there is only one significant reference to memory, a quotation from the works of Harphius (Henry Herp), which Baker translates with approval and, in effect, makes his own. The passage is interesting, for it illustrates some of the practical consequences that contemplation was supposed to have on the mind, particularly in unifying and elevating the various faculties and powers:

By the consurrection or elevation of the superior soul the memory is at length, after a long exercise, made in itself quiet, clear, and calm in her conversion towards divine things and pure from all foreign images; because she is elevated above all sensitive and imaginary things, and above all things that might hinder her in such conversion or application of herself towards God. And she is brought to be firm and stable in unity of spirit; and all the powers both inferior and superior are brought up into the same unity of spirit; and so they are raised and heaved up above all multiplicity, distractions, thoughts, and occupations, as if a man were elevated above the clouds into a true clear tranquillity, where neither wind, nor clouds, nor hail, nor rain can reach, and where there is no manner of change. And so the memory is brought into so admirably clear a tranquillity and quietness that it were not credible or intelligible to a man that had not experienced it;

by which clear infused light and tranquillity the man finds himself recollected and established, and that he has pierced through and is anchored in the unity of his spirit; the which unity and quietness he doth now possess even at his proper mansion or dwelling-place, as if he were a man of heaven and not of this life. (*Commentary*, 179)

The phrase "unity of spirit," repeated three or four times, suggests Baker's center or point of the spirit.

II   *The Faculties in Contemplation*

Concern with contemplation is even older than faculty psychology. Aristotle, in the *Nicomachean Ethics*, followed the lead of Plato in giving precedence to the contemplative, intellectual life. "The activity of God, which surpasses all others in blessedness, must be contemplative; and of human activities, therefore, that which is most akin to this must be most of the nature of happiness." [13] The Classical philosophers, however, thought of contemplation as a rational process, as the use of man's reason to discover the truth of the universe. Christian thinkers who followed could not put so much trust in unaided reason, and some went so far as to say that reason should be entirely abandoned in the contemplative search for God.

Dionysius, the earliest and most influential mystic in this tradition, wrote: "Man must plunge into the mystical darkness of Unknowing in which he lays aside all rational knowledge and becomes absorbed in that which is wholly intangible and invisible . . . so that he is united to that which is wholly unknowable by the highest part of the mind in the complete cessation of rational knowledge and knows in a manner beyond mind by knowing nothing." [14] Dionysius was interpreted, in a commentary by Vercellensis on the *Mystical Theology*, to mean that understanding should be replaced by will:

For they [the pagan philosophers] thought that the highest cognitive faculty was the intellect, whereas there is another which as far excels the intellect as the intellect does the reason, or the reason the imagination; and this is the higher will (*principalis affectio*), and the same is the spark of conscience (*scintilla synderesis*) which alone may be united to the divine Spirit. . . . In this exercise sense, imagination, reason, and intellect are suspended . . . and the point of the higher will (*apex affectionis principalis*) is united to the divine Spirit itself. . . . This is the *best part* of Mary. . . . This wisdom is obtained by a great fervour of love towards God and a strong straining of the spirit towards the eternal objects of wisdom (*aeterna spectacula sapientiae*).[15]

Even St. Augustine—who elsewhere balances understanding, memory, and will—wrote, in one of those frequent unqualified statements scattered through his works that do not seem to represent his considered opinion, *"nihil aliud sumus quam voluntates"* (we are nothing but wills).[16] According to Hugh of St. Victor, *"Ibi non intrat intellectus, sed affectus"* (here enters not the intellect but the will), and both St. Bernard and St. Bonaventure agree that love, a function of will, goes where reason cannot.[17]

In the words of Justin McCann, however, "a more temperate school . . . holding fast to the doctrine that there is no willing without knowing . . . refused to depose the intellect." [18] St. Thomas states that "truth is the end of contemplation"; but for this very reason "it has the aspect of an appetible good," and so is to be approached by both the will and the understanding.[19] In a passage which considers the claims to superiority of intellect and will over each other, he writes:

The superiority of one thing over another can be considered in two ways: *absolutely* and *relatively*. . . . If therefore the intellect and will be considered with regard to themselves, then the intellect is the higher power. And this is clear if we compare their respective objects to one another. For the object of the intellect is more simple and more absolute than the object of the will; since the object of the intellect is the very idea of appetible good; and the appetible good, the idea of which is in the intellect, is the object of the will. . . . But relatively and by comparison with something else, we find that the will is sometimes higher than the intellect, from the fact that the object of the will occurs in something higher than that in which occurs the object of the intellect. . . . When, therefore, the thing in which there is good is nobler than the soul itself, in which is the idea understood; by comparison with such a thing, the will is higher than the intellect. But when the thing which is good is less noble than the soul, then even in comparison with that thing the intellect is higher than the will. Wherefore the love of God is better than the knowledge of God; but, on the contrary, the knowledge of corporeal things is better than the love thereof. Absolutely, however, the intellect is nobler than the will.[20]

This Thomistic position helps to reconcile what seem at first to be conflicting opinions among the scholastic and the mystical writers; for it is clear that, when Dionysius advises the abandonment of reason, he is talking about a different realm from the everyday world, in which reason has its valid uses. Even a mystic recognizes the place of reason in ordinary affairs, while Aquinas in turn recognizes the limitations of the intellect in directly approaching God.

III *Rationalism and Voluntarism*

In England in the sixteenth and seventeenth centuries, the argument as to the relative importance of reason and will in religious matters became particularly important because many of the sectarians in opposition to the Established Church decried reason and claimed that the will of God, or the inspired will of the Elect, was the only proper guide. Calvin's God was pure will, above all human attributes of justice or reason or order: he did not do what He did because it was good; it was good because He did it. Some of the enthusiasts of the period, feeling themselves inspired by God, arrogated God's super-rationality to themselves. As a result of this religious voluntarism, writers who favored the Establishment grew suspicious of will and stressed order and rationality. Shakespeare, who reflects so many of the currents of his age, invariably makes his self-willed men villains—Iago, Edmund, or Richard III—while his approval is extended to order, cooperation, and corporate responsibility. Milton's Satan, who boasts of his "unconquerable will," is another individualistic villain who puts self-will above order and reason. All the commonplaces that E. M. W. Tillyard has gathered together in *The Elizabethan World Picture* (1944) show the universality and the complexity of this conception of world order—a picture which was largely inherited from scholasticism but which was becoming increasingly elaborated and hardened in opposition to the growing currents of religious voluntarism, as well as to the later draining of value from the natural world which accompanied the scientific revolution.

In addition to the growth of religious voluntarism and anti-intellectualism, there was in the Renaissance a more worldly kind of voluntarism expressed in the precepts of Machiavelli or the Italian ideal of *virtù;* it is seen in Marlowe's heroes and in the lives of the self-made men of the Elizabethan court. In England, voluntarism owed something to the Tudor and Stuart policy of replacing the old courtiers with new men; self-aggrandizement and meteoric rise to power received royal sanction. The dream of power found new forms and infected the unlikeliest men, so that Edmund Spenser pursued the hope of high position at court and Francis Bacon debased his talents even while he channeled the same dream of power into the new science. The effect that these two kinds of voluntarism, religious and secular, had upon the more traditional or conservative writers was to put will into disrepute. Instead of identifying it with divine love, its highest expression, they most often equated it with selfishness and pride. The conception of free will was endangered by the reaction from unbridled voluntarism, by predestinarian theories, and by its old enemy astrology, which experienced a new popularity.

In this climate of ideas Hooker, the spokesman for Anglicanism, tried to define will in such a way that his Puritan adversaries could not use it to support their position; in effect, he makes will totally dependent upon reason:

The Will, properly and strictly taken . . . differeth greatly from that inferior natural desire which we call Appetite. The object of Appetite is whatsoever sensible good may be wished for; the object of Will is that good which Reason doth lead us to seek. . . . Finally, Appetite is the Will's solicitor, and the Will is Appetite's controller; what we covet according to the one by the other we often reject; neither is any other desire termed properly Will, but that where Reason and Understanding, or the show of Reason, prescribeth the thing desired.[21]

Elsewhere, speaking of the claims of the enthusiasts, Hooker writes: "It is not therefore the fervent earnestness of their persuasion, but the soundness of those reasons whereupon the same is built, which must declare their opinions . . . wrought by the Holy Ghost." [22] The appeal is not from erroneous self-will to will corrected and guided by grace, but to reason.

Hooker's aversion to the expression of personal opinions in religion and to the willfulness of the sects led him to make a well-known statement that embodies all the desire of the conservative Elizabethan for conformity, for the corporate unity of the state, and for an end to the unbridled expression of individual will: "The general and perpetual voice of men is as the sentence of God himself. For that which all men have at all times learned, Nature herself must needs have taught; and God being the author of Nature, her voice is but his instrument." [23]

This view is, at least, not egotistical. It is, moreover, a wonderful expression of the Elizabeth passion for order. Nevertheless, the statement that "the general and perpetual voice of men is as the sentence of God himself" is a strong one with implications of conformity that go beyond the normal respect of a conservative Christian for tradition. Hooker gives the impression, here at least, that God, the moving principle behind nature, works only through the whole of humanity, and that the idea of God speaking to the individual soul must be abandoned. Whether Hooker would have explicitly supported such a position is doubtful; but, in his effort to combat the individualistic extremes of the enthusiasts and to reverse the trend of the Puritan element in the Church toward a private, charismatic religion, he assumes a position that leaves little room for personal inspiration or for the exercise of the individual will. Will, rightly used, is subordinate to reason; and reason in turn is a manifestation of the universal order of creation and of mankind in general.

Hobbes thought that Hooker and the scholastic philosophers coupled will and reason too closely. Since in Hobbes's view the universe was entirely made up of matter in motion, and spirit was a meaningless concept, it was natural for him to deny the existence of anything like the higher will of the scholastics. Will was, in fact, nothing but appetite: "In *Deliberation,* the last Appetite, or Aversion, immediately adhaering to the action, or to the omission thereof, is that wee call the wɪʟʟ; the Act, (not the faculty,) of *Willing.* And Beasts that have *Deliberation,* must necessarily also have Will. The Definition of the *Will,* given commonly by the Schooles, that it is a Rationall Appetite, is not good. For if it were, then could there be no Voluntary Act against Reason. . . . *Will therefore is the last Appetite in Deliberating.*" [24] Thus will was attacked from yet another angle; either it was so rational that, when it was properly used, it was entirely subordinated to reason, or it was an animal appetite that had to be kept forcibly in check by the commonwealth for the protection of its members.

While these currents of voluntarism and rationalistic antivoluntarism were developing in English thought, the writings of many of the Catholics of the period still echoed older traditions, of which two are pertinent. One is the attitude toward will, previously mentioned, that was expressed by the mystics from Dionysius through Bernard and Bonaventura, down into the mystical revival of the sixteenth and seventeenth centuries. In the view of the mystic, the will is important because it, rather than the understanding, is the faculty best fitted to approach God. The understanding, however, is dismissed entirely by only a few extremists; for most mystics, it follows or accompanies the will, acting through the medium of faith. The other tradition is the attitude of the scholastic theologians, who view will chiefly as one of the intellectual faculties. While some of the theologians, like Hooker, effectively subordinated the will to the reason most preferred, like St. Thomas, to balance them.

Although these two traditions differ in emphasis, they do not necessarily disagree; and it is possible to find both echoed in a single writer. The following passage, which is in essential agreement with Baker's position, is from the writings of an anonymous Spanish mystic who lived shortly before him. There are obvious reflections of both traditions:

In this life the union of the will [with God] is far more excellent than the union of the understanding, and it is better to love God than to know Him, because that which we can love with the will is much more than that which we can attain with the understanding. The reason for this may be gathered from a consideration of the respective modes of operation of the understanding and the will. . . . When the understanding understands, it . . . forms an idea of it within itself. . . . Since its capacity is finite, it reduces within its own limitations the object understood. . . . The will, on the contrary, when it loves goes out of itself and is transformed into the object loved and is made one thing with it. The object loved is not therefore limited by it.[25]

The explanation of why will is superior to understanding when the object is God exactly parallels the passage from St. Thomas. When the writer talks of being transformed into God and becoming one with Him, however, he is leaving the realm of ordinary theology and entering the Dionysian tradition of mysticism, the unitive way.

IV *Baker's Exercise of the Will*

The emphasis that Baker puts on the faculty of will was apparent in the discussion in Chapter 3 of forced acts of the will and the prayer of aspirations. David Knowles, in an early study of Baker, wrote: "The understanding, he holds, can do no more than set the will, find the target, and calculate the range. When this has been done, it must retire." [26] This interpretation is not entirely accurate, because the understanding has a continuing, if limited, part to play in Baker's theory of contemplation; but it is a good first approximation. Baker's teachings about the will apply primarily to contemplation—in its broadest sense, including the preparatory stages—and contemplation in turn he defined by the exercise of the will. He considered that meditation was particularly characterized by the exercise of understanding and its related virtue, faith, while contemplation was increasingly characterized by the exercise of the will, particularly in love. This is one reason why, although (as Baker well knew) the true division between mystical and non-mystical prayer is between his forced acts and his aspirations, he nevertheless makes another major division between meditation and forced acts. A passage from the *Confessions* illustrates this fact: "A soul that by a divine call, as being in a state of maturity for it, relinquisheth meditation to the end to betake herself to a more sublime exercise, which is that of immediate acts or affections of the will, then only begins to enter into the ways of contemplation. For the exercises of the will are the sublimest that any soul can practice." [27] A key phrase is "the ways of contemplation," a term Baker ordinarily uses to include the preparatory stage of acts of the will as well as true contemplation.

Occasionally, Baker simply uses "contemplation" to include this whole range of prayers, but he does so merely as a convenience since he shows clearly enough in a number of passages that he does not consider the prayer of acts to be mystical. In *Sancta Sophia*, for example, he distinguishes three general classes of mental prayer: "1. Discursive prayer or meditation. 2. The prayer of forced immediate acts or affections of the will, without discourse preparatory thereto. 3. The prayer of pure active contemplation or aspirations, as it were naturally and without any force flowing from the soul, powerfully and immediately directed and moved by the Holy Spirit. Now this third degree . . . is, indeed, truly the prayer of contemplation" (3.2.1.5).

According to David Knowles, Baker, "who was well aware of the elementary part played by the imagination and the reason in prayer, failed to see clearly that in the realm of the will his 'forced acts' were equally elementary. . . . Fr Baker, therefore, is at fault when he describes the prayer of the will, *tout court*, as 'contemplative.'" [28] Baker does not, in fact, make this mistake; he occasionally uses the word "contemplative" loosely, to include the stages preparatory to mystical prayer, but he usually speaks of the "paths" or "ways" of contemplation when he intends to include forced acts, and in any case his meaning must be determined by the context.

The distinction between Baker's first stage of prayer and the two higher stages is the distinction between discursive prayer and prayer of the will. The first two stages, however, resemble each other in that they are both produced by the efforts of the individual soul, while the third stage, true contemplation, flows without effort "and without any force" by the agency of the Holy Spirit. Although Baker felt that acts and aspirations were both predominantly concerned with the will, he did not confuse the laborious prayer of acts with true mysticism.

All mystics, according to Baker, agree that will has an important part to play in the contemplative way and in the direct approach to God: a view that Dionysius, Hugh of St. Victor, and St. Thomas support. One of the first premises of most mystics is that only love, which is in the will, [29] can unite the soul with God. St. Bernard, for example, in his *Sermones in Cantica Canticorum*, writes that without love the reader of this work will understand nothing that he says: "For love speaks in it everywhere; if anyone would understand the things he reads in it, then let him love." "Without love," says Hugh of St. Victor to his soul, "you cannot exist." [30] The allegory of Christ as the bridegroom and the soul as the bride is one of the commonest in Christian mystical literature; love and not knowledge or reason unites the soul to God.

When Baker considers the lower stages of prayer, he speaks of various aspects of the will: acts of sorrow and contrition for sins, or of resignation to God. He speaks less of love than many mystics, partly because his method is as far as possible reasoned and discursive, using few images or appeals to the emotions. There are, nevertheless, many passages that show that he identifies the highest states of prayer with the exercise of love (again divorcing "exercise" of its active connotations, since in this prayer God is the real agent). We may permit one passage from *Sancta Sophia* to speak for the rest: "In regard of the will: it is in this exercise so wholly possessed and inflamed with divine love, which doth so intimely penetrate into the very centre of it, that it is become like fiery, burning steel, clean through shining with this fire. It is now a will deiform, and in a manner deified, for it is so closely united and hidden in the Divine Will, that God may be said to will and do all things in and by her" (3.4.2.26). Purgative acts of will, like contrition, are ordinarily left behind, as the soul progresses, even before making the change from forced acts to aspirations; and, in the higher stages of prayer, the will is filled with love, conforming itself to the will of God, which is also love.

Baker is, therefore, in the main contemplative tradition when he writes: "For the first they [all mystics] agree in this: that [in contemplation] all that the soul doth is by the will: I mean that it is the will that goes foremost and makes the breach and the understanding doth but follow or at least accompany the will. The will is the guide and captain, and the understanding doth but attend the will, going whither he goes and following him" (*Confessions*, 91).

The understanding, although it is incapable of leading the way in these realms, accompanies the will, and perceives what the will has led it to by a kind of blind faith: "Secondly, the understanding so accompanying the will is to carry with it no images or species of created things . . . but . . . only to retain an apprehension and memory of God according to that totality that our faith tells of Him. And such knowledge retained of God is by the removing of all created things from Him, which done there remaineth as it were nothing, the which nothing is all that we can know of Him in this life" (*Confessions*, 91–92).

V *The Will and Imageless Contemplation*

Baker, like the scholastic psychologists, believed that the understanding could not normally operate without the use of symbols or phantasms—or, as a modern linguist might put it, it is impossible to think without using language in some form.[31] Therefore, in natural terms, the understanding perceives "nothing" in contemplation; nevertheless, this nothing is "the nearest sight that we have in this life of God" (*Confessions,* 92) and is therefore more to be valued as closer to the ultimate truth than any of the images that derive from created things and that make up the ordinary furniture of the mind. It is "the most perfect and most angelical knowing that a soul is capable of in this life" (*Sancta Sophia,* 3.4.2.25).

Again and again Baker speaks of the need to rise above the use of images, to abandon the reflections of creation in the mind, and to approach God in the darkness of faith. In one place he even defines contemplation by its characteristic of rising above imagery: "What contemplatives mean by the term 'contemplation' is the regard of the Divinity immediately and above all particular images, and is called in our holy Rule 'pure prayer.'" [32] Images come between the soul and God, but in true contemplation the soul views and approaches God "immediately." As prayer grows more sublime, so do the images in the mind during recollection grow fewer and more subtle. In the darkness of Active Union, as Baker employs the term, all imagery is abandoned. The soul is "without any image and above all images . . . there is . . . neither time nor place nor image, but a certain vacuity or emptiness." [33] In speaking of union, he constantly uses the term "imageless" and implies that at the highest levels of prayer images are entirely abandoned.

There are, however, several brief passages in *Sancta Sophia* in which Baker expresses doubt as to whether the use of phantasms can ever be entirely done away with:

But a soul, after a long practice of internal abstraction and renouncing of all representations of God, contents herself with such a confused notion of Him as may be apprehended by an obscure general faith; that is to say, not simply and absolutely with no kind of image at all (for that is supposed inconsistent with the operations of the soul whilst it is in a mortal body), but not with a distinct, formal, chosen, particular image.[34] (3.4.2.6)

This passage, together with a few others, appears to be a retreat from Baker's often-repeated goal of transcending all imagery; and it contradicts what he says elsewhere. It is in agreement with the opinions of Aristotle and St. Thomas, who both wrote that the intellect can understand nothing without the use of phantasms. Most mystical writers, however, thought that this limitation on the soul did not apply in the case of true mysticism, which transcends normal psychological processes.[35] Although mystical experiences must afterward be translated into human imagery when the contemplative reflects upon them or passes them on to others, they are at the time of their actual occurrence imageless; in mystical union the soul approaches God in a region above the discursive understanding. This opinion is Baker's usual one, but he seems to make a "concession to the 'Schools' " [36] in these passages; it is as if, while he himself felt that contemplation was imageless, he did not like to contradict the opinion of the scholastic philosophers.

One of the advantages of imageless contemplation is that in this kind of prayer the contemplative is not open to the corruptive influence of the senses, the imagination, or the discursive reason— all damaged by the consequences of the fall. Neither is the mystic subject to temptations or illusions caused by the devil, as long as he remains in the region of the soul above the individual powers. According to traditional belief, only God can read minds; and angels (or devils) are therefore limited to the perception and manipulation of the senses, the sensitive appetites, and the imagination.[37] This belief, together with the doctrine of the fallibility of human reason after the fall, was in Baker's mind when he wrote concerning the contemplative who has risen above the use of images: "What possibility of illusion or error can there be to such a soul?" (*Sancta Sophia*, 1.1.3.2). In lower states of prayer, illusions can be mistaken for the guidance of God; but this error is no longer possible in true contemplation.

Rising above imagery involves a kind of spiritualizing process, drawing the center of the soul's activities up from the lower functions of the senses and the imagination, either into the intellectual powers of the reason, memory, and will, or into the higher point of the spirit. The passions are replaced by a calm perseverance. In the *Commentary*, Baker redefines the "vehement and languishing desire towards God"—which the author of the *Cloud* considers so important to the contemplative—as "a resolute and quiet determination of the superior will that will not give over seeking God for any difficulty whatsoever, and especially for any troublesome importunity of distractive thoughts" (202). Here we see the need for pure will unalloyed by passions: for a steady, driving determination in the approach to God.

Although Baker constantly stresses the use of the will in con-

templation, he is not a voluntarist in the usual sense. He believed
that the understanding must accompany the will in its journey
toward God, and nowhere does he echo St. Augustine's words
about man's being nothing but will. Although will leads the way,
contemplation involves all the faculties. Baker writes in one place
that true contemplation "is meerly and only in the powers of the
superior soul, viz. memory, will, and understanding." [38] In many
other places he speaks of contemplation as taking place in the
"higher powers" of the soul. Concerning the highest kind of contemplation, such as St. Paul's rapture to the third heaven, Baker
writes: "The exercise of these men doth pass in the height or top
of the spirit—if you will admit any such thing to be in a man's
soul—that is, above the powers of it" (*Commentary*, 177). The
"powers," of course, are the three faculties.

Whenever Baker speaks of the height of the spirit, it is defen-
sively and apologetically, as if he had been involved in some controversy on this point, the details of which are not preserved.[39] For
this reason perhaps he did not more often qualify his doctrine of
the will by speaking of the unifying point of the soul above the
faculties. The doctrine, found in the writings of many of the
Rhineland mystics, is orthodox; in fact, St. John of the Cross, who
goes much further than Baker, writes that the center of the soul is
not only the point of contact with God, but at its very center actually *is* God.[40] This point may seem abstruse, but the practical con-
sequence of the belief in the existence of such a center is that none
of the faculties is given absolute precedence over the other; and
the extremes of voluntarism or rationalism are avoided.

VI   *Mysticism and Humanism*

If Baker did not eliminate understanding from the contemplative way, he was even further from disparaging its importance in
ordinary life and in the approaches to contemplation. According
to Robert Hoopes, "the intellectual history of the seventeenth century is marked by the gradual dissociation of knowledge and virtue as accepted and indivisible elements in the ideal structure of
human reason, a shift from the tradition of right reason to the new
tradition of scientific reasoning." [41] In the struggle between Christian humanism and science, in which the religious voluntarists and
extremists aided science by disparaging reason and dissociating it
from belief, Baker was on many points an ally of the humanists—

although, as a Catholic exile, he played no direct part in the controversy. The doctrine of right reason, which is central to Christian humanism, fuses knowing with doing; it states that one must do well in order to know, and that one must know in order to do well. In other words, "what a man knows depends upon what, as a moral being, he chooses to make himself." [42]

It may seem improper to group a mystic with Christian humanists; in fact, through a misapprehension mysticism was in low repute among the English Protestant humanists. Although contemplation was, for Baker and other Catholic mystics, not mere theory or speculative philosophy, but a practical way of life, it lost this meaning for the English humanists. Contemplation was reduced in meaning to secular study and intellectual curiosity; therefore, the active life was preferred on moral as well as on practical grounds. According to Howard Schultz, Hall's definition of the slothful man reveals the prejudice of his fellow English Protestants: "He is a religious man, and wears the time in his cloister; and as the cloak of his doing nothing, pleads contemplation." [43] Baker, however, felt that in contemplation he was doing what was most worth while: he was approaching God as directly as possible.

Although right reason is moderate in balancing virtue and knowledge, it need not be moderate in its ultimate aims. A passage from Plato shows how, for the humanist, knowing depends on moral considerations: "Just as one might have to turn the whole body round in order that the eye should see light instead of darkness, so the entire soul must be turned away from this changing world, until its eye can bear to contemplate reality and that supreme splendour which we have called the Good." In another passage, Plato writes: "We ought to fly away from earth to heaven as quickly as we can; and to fly away is to become like God, as far as this is possible; and to become like him, is to become holy, just, and wise." [44]

The same equation and interaction of wisdom and virtue are found in Baker's teachings, and neither of these passages would appear out of place in *Sancta Sophia*. The humanist and the mystic, then, need not be in opposition to each other, although the mystic is concerned with a more specialized field of human activity. Historically, mystics and pseudo-mystics have been suspicious of the rationalistic side of humanism; and humanists have been suspicious of mysticism; but the conflict is not inherent in their respective views of life, nor is it impossible, as can be seen in the *Summa Theologica*, to imagine a metaphysics in which both rationalism and mysticism have their place. It is not always noticed, for example, that there is a highly mystical conclusion to a famous passage in Pico della Mirandola's *Oratio de dignitate hominis*, usually considered one of the seminal manifestoes of humanism and of the Renaissance belief in man's greatness:

When man came into life, the Father endowed him with all kinds of seeds and with the germs of every way of life. Whatever seeds each man cultivates will grow and bear fruit in him. If these seeds are vegetative, he will be like a plant; if they are sensitive, he will become like the beasts; if they are rational, he will become like a heavenly creature; if intellectual, he will be an angel and a son of God. And if, content with the lot of no created being, he withdraws into the centre of his own oneness, his spirit, made one with God in the solitary darkness of the Father, which is above all things, will surpass all things.[45]

The "centre of his own oneness" is almost undoubtedly the point of the spirit or *scintilla synderesis* of the mystics; and to be "made one with God in the solitary darkness of the Father" speaks for itself.

Baker felt that it was impossible to write usefully about mysticism without having personally experienced it. This attitude is not an obscurantist attack on the value of learning or knowledge; it parallels the conviction of the Christian humanist that only the man who lives well can be truly wise. Milton, always a supporter of reason, believed that philosophy and theory had their roots in practice; in order to be a poet a man "ought him selfe to bee a true Poem"; and for a man to "be truly eloquent who is not withall a good man" is impossible.[46]

Baker believed that prayer, in addition to rectifying the will and strengthening the virtues, also gave the contemplative wisdom and enlightenment. John Worthington, in a letter to Henry More, the Cambridge Platonist, spoke with approval of Baker's "discovery of selfness and nature in her many close interests and designs, and most secret insinuations." [47] He might easily have been referring to passages like the following, which parallels the humanist assumption that intellectual illumination goes along with virtuous action:

> Those that use their imagination and discourse do not perceive the hidden impediments between themselves and God, for it is the regarding of God and His presence, and not the consideration of creatures and their images, that enlightens the soul and enables her to see her hidden inordinate affections. More palpable sins the soul can perceive by her internal senses and natural reason, and these she can amend. But the root or affection remains unseen, unknown, and will again break out into act when the soul least expects it. (*Inner Life*, 147)

Worthington did not agree with Baker's mystical overtones, but the assumption that wisdom and action are interconnected is held by both men; the difference between them on this point is that for Baker practical action includes the approach to God by contemplation. Both humanist and mystic would have agreed with St. Ignatius when he wrote that "it is not an abundance of knowledge that fills and satisfies the soul but rather an interior understanding and savoring of things." [48]

Baker believed that in contemplation, experience is more important than learning and courageous will more important than reasoning power. A strong statement in support of this belief is to be found in *Sancta Sophia:*

> Now, for a further proof of the excellency and security of contemplative prayer beyond active, experience demonstrates that all the most sublime exercises of contemplation may as purely and perfectly be performed by persons the most ignorant and unlearned (so they be sufficiently instructed in the fundamental doctrines of Catholic faith) as by the learnedst doctors, inasmuch as not any abilities in the brain are requisite thereto, but only a strong courageous affection of the heart. Hence it is that we see that simple unlearned women are more frequently graced by Almighty God with the gift of high contemplation than men, and especially such men as are much given to sublime speculations. (1.1.3.3.)

Elsewhere in *Sancta Sophia* Baker writes that, according to the great mystics, "no trust is to be given to learning without experience, but much to experience though without learning" and that "no learning, therefore, that may be got by study and reading, though of all the contemplative books that now are extant, will alone serve to enable any one to be a competent director for internal livers" (1.2.2.5,6). The use of the qualifying word "alone" should be noted: Baker does not say that reading and learning are profitless for the contemplative, but that they must supplement action and experience.

Books are to be used as they are appropriate to a person's character and to his degree of advancement in contemplation. If a soul conforms to divine guidance, "no knowledge would hurt her; yea, rather it would be a help, if not to her, at least to others" (*Inner Life*, 21). Only that knowledge that can be inwardly absorbed is profitable; and the beginning contemplative should avoid cramming himself full of theories which have no pertinence to his state in life. Used properly, books can be useful: "Observe your own way, spirit, and call; and of books, take and practise according as you shall find to be proper and answerable to such way, spirit, and call of yours; and no more or further. And doing so, you may almost by all kinds of spiritual books receive comfort, or other good, and no manner of harm" (*Commentary*, 154).

Baker's letter to Sir Robert Cotton pleading for books for the nuns of Cambray, his own spiritual reading, and his voluminous writings are evidence that he did not undervalue books or learning. His attitude toward the use of books is exemplified by his advice to the nuns of Cambray that they read *The Cloud of Unknowing* several times over, every two years: "and I hope you will every time understand it better than you did before" (*Commentary*, 155). In other words, their growth through practical experience will increase their capacity for learning, and doing and knowing will interact.

Baker's commonsense approach to faculty psychology and his refusal to give any one element sole pre-eminence in the approach to contemplation—whether will or reason, experience or learning —are characteristic of his moderate, balanced approach to mysticism and to the psychology and methodology of religious growth. When he stresses one element, such as will, it is to combat what seems to him a popular excess in the other direction. In the case of will, this excess results from the spreading popularity of the meditative book, particularly the Ignatian *Exercises*, which he felt advocated an overelaborate and overintellectualized approach to spirituality (*Sancta Sophia,* 1.2.2.15). The emphasis on experience as opposed to learning is likewise due in part to his acquaintance with men like Fr. Rudisind Barlow, who were trained in theology but lacked any feeling for personal devotion. Pedantry and useless learning are the legitimate targets even for the intellectual.

One notable aspect of Baker's method of prayer is that it outlines a devotion open to the unlearned and the unintellectual. It was noted in the last chapter that the four methods of prayer that he suggests as approaches to contemplation enable people of widely differing character and diverse talents to approach the mystical way in the manner that best fits them. By stressing the importance of will and experience, supplemented as far as possible or as appropriate with learning, Baker suggests a kind of devotion open to anyone with courage and perseverance. St. Thomas, near the beginning of the *Summa Contra Gentiles,* wrote: "If the only way open to us for the knowledge of God were solely that of reason, the human race would remain in the blackest shadows of ignorance. For then the knowledge of God, which especially renders men perfect and good, would come to be possessed only by a few, and these few would require a great deal of time in order to reach it." [49]

St. Thomas was speaking of the need for revelation, but the passage has a relevance to Baker's teachings and to his belief that the deepest kind of prayer is not approached by reason or by learning, although these may help and should not be neglected, but by moral courage and strength of will.

CHAPTER 5

Inspiration

I *The Issue of Inspiration*

THE controversy between Baker and Fr. Hull, as well as the later disputes while Baker was at Douay, indicate that during his lifetime his teachings were most criticized because of his doctrine of divine calls, together with the related question of obedience to authority. That this dispute continued after his death is made clear by, among other things, Cressy's preface to *Sancta Sophia*, which devotes a full twenty pages to explaining and defending Baker's teachings about inspiration. In fact, Cressy notes elsewhere, that, although he omitted several appendixes from *Sancta Sophia* to avoid "too great a proportion and bulk," it "was judged very expedient and almost necessary" to retain the defense of the doctrine of inspiration.[1] While Cressy denies that Baker's orthodoxy was ever in question, he acknowledges that this one aspect of *Sancta Sophia* needs a defense. Near the beginning of his preface he writes:

This is to acquaint thee that the *immaculate doctrine* contained in this book, though it never met with any that opposed, or so much as questioned, the verities thereof, speculatively considered, yet there have not wanted some that have judged them not fit to be thus exposed to thy view, much doubting thou wouldst prove such an one as would make an ill use and perverse advantage from them.

Now the principal, yea only, point that gives some this jealousy is that which thou wilt find in the *Second Section* of the *First Treatise*, where is treated touching divine illuminations, inspirations, impulses, and other secret operations of God's Holy Spirit in the hearts of internal livers. (Pref. 2–3)

As Cressy points out, there was no doubt of the theoretical orthodoxy of Baker's doctrine; but there was some dispute how prudent it would be to publish teachings so open to misinterpretation.

The issue of personal inspiration was extremely important, since it was used by many of the Protestant sects and by some Catholics as well (such as the Illuminists and Quietists) to deny the authority of church laws or hierarchies and, in some extreme cases, that of the Bible itself. The political implications of these theories were fully as significant as the religious. In England even more than in the Catholic countries—because the king was the head of the church and the church was national—government was tied to ecclesiastical structure, so that there was good reason to say "No bishop, no king."

McCann, in an article about opposition to Baker's doctrines during the years immediately preceding publication of *Sancta Sophia*, writes that there were "those who, while not impugning the orthodoxy of the teaching, considered that it was open to misconstruction by heretics or by ignorant Catholics. There would seem in fact to have been a party of 'inopportunists' definitely opposed on such prudential grounds to the publication of the teaching." [2] Cressy says that it was feared that some of the "fanatic sectaries" in England would take advantage of the doctrine of inspiration to justify their "frenzies and disorders" (*Sancta Sophia*, Pref. 21); and he presumably has in mind such sects as the Ranters, or perhaps the Quakers, though neither Catholics nor Protestants distinguished very carefully among their opponents. One Quaker apologist, Robert Barclay, did make use of Baker's doctrine, misquoting him so as to make it appear that Baker opposed masses, confession, devotion to saints, or any other limitations on spiritual freedom.[3] Barclay also says that Baker and earlier Catholic mystics formed a "sect" in the Catholic Church and that they were forerunners of the Quakers in the development of an interior, personal religion that was free from hierarchy or ritual. He is, however, the only one to take advantage of Baker's teachings.

Cressy argues that those who object to the publication of Baker's doctrine are short-sighted and that it will better serve Catholicism to publish it than to try to deny that inspiration exists. "For what other way," he writes, "does there remain to convince them of their errors. . . . Shall we tell them that there are no inspirations at all? We shall, in so doing, betray the Christian religion." It will always be possible for anyone so minded "to draw poison from the most perfect doctrines of Catholic Faith" (Pref. 31, 32), but it would be a grave error to leave all teaching on the subject of inspiration in the hands of the sectaries. The doctrine of divine inspiration is "the very soul of Christianity," found in the writings of all the mystics and most of the Fathers. It is taught in the schools, where it is fully approved; but "meeting with it thus popularly spread" for the "use and practice of the unlearned," the objectors now have second thoughts, fearing that what is right in theory may prove dangerous in practice (Pref. 5).

Post-Reformation Catholicism had been forced into a defensive posture by the attacks of the reformers; and, while Baker's period witnessed a reaction against this reaction, with a new spirituality brought into the Church by such figures as St. Ignatius and St. Teresa, nevertheless the exigencies of polemic and the fear of new incursions by the reformers still remained. Particularly with regard to inspiration and personal religion, the response to sectarian extremes had made it difficult to think dispassionately or to discuss the subject in print without overreacting to Protestant interpretations.

It was Baker's virtue that he was able to ignore these crosscurrents, that he refused to be pushed into a false position by his adversaries. Just as he was able to engage in the seemingly remote activity of antiquarian research in England, while all around him Catholics were persecuted and he himself was always in danger of arrest, so he was able to discuss the subject of inspiration without being disturbed by the polemical atmosphere that surrounded this topic. Although he advocated nothing not previously suggested by the Fathers or by earlier mystics, it was highly original in his time for anyone to return to the Fathers on this point, to rise above current preoccupations and to bring the subject of inspiration back into its traditional perspective.

Most commentaries on Baker agree that his treatment of inspiration and divine calls is, in spite of its orthodoxy, probably the most original and valuable aspect of his work.[4] It is, like the rest of his doctrines in *Sancta Sophia,* intended for contemplatives; and he warns other Christians "not at all to meddle with instructions belonging to contemplation" but to make use of "the precepts and exercises of an active life . . . in order to the end thereof, the perfection of external Christian charity" (1.2.3.4). In spite of this caution, however, his doctrine obviously has implications that go beyond the contemplative life. His arguments for inner freedom for the contemplative inevitably suggest that even the active man must be spiritually free: that, like the contemplative, and within the framework of religious and social order, the active man must follow his conscience, and obey what Protestants called "the Gospel of the heart." Since Baker was chiefly concerned with the part that divine calls played in the mystical life, this discussion is for the most part limited to that area; but the general implication of what he says is more widely pertinent, whether or not he intended it to be so.

II Baker's Doctrine of Inspiration

It has been the traditional Christian teaching—repeatedly asserted by St. Paul, for example—that all Christians receive sufficient grace and enlightenment to meet whatever temptations they face. In Baker's words, "the light and virtue of common grace afford generally, to all good Christians that seriously endeavor to save their souls, such internal illuminations and motions as are sufficient to direct them for the resisting of any sinful temptation, or to perform any necessary act of virtue, in circumstances wherein they are obliged" (*Sancta Sophia*, 1.2.1.8). This grace enables anyone willing to cooperate with it to perform the minimum requirements for salvation, or, in case of a fall, to repent with sufficient sorrow for forgiveness.

Anyone not satisfied with a life that merely meets the minimum requirements—and this must particularly include the contemplative—must strive to obey the counsel of perfection: "Be ye perfect, as your heavenly Father is perfect." In fact, anyone becoming a religious "obliges himself to seek perfection" (*Sancta Sophia*, 1.3.4.1). But, because all the faculties and powers of man have been weakened by the fall, guidance is necessary to avoid going astray: "For certainly a guide must needs be had, since it is evident that in our present state of corrupt nature, we have no light so much as to discover that there is any such way, and much less to direct and enable us to walk in paths so much above, yea, so directly contrary to the designs and interests of nature" (1.2.1.1). The Scriptures, the doctrines of the Church, even the individually tailored advice of a spiritual director are insufficient in themselves to lead the soul to perfection. Outward conformity to law and precept is not enough, for there must also be a perfect interior conformity and a cheerful willingness accompanying every action. The only guide that can direct the soul in these paths is the Holy Spirit—whether through external events and persons, or by direct interior inspiration.

The passage in *Sancta Sophia* in which Baker argues the necessity of divine guidance is lengthy, but it is so important for a proper understanding of his doctrine of inspiration and so central to his whole approach to spirituality that it is worth quoting the significant part of it in full:

From these unquestionable grounds thus truly laid, it follows evidently that in all good actions, and especially in the internal ways of the spirit which conduct to contemplation and perfection, God alone is our only master and director; and creatures, when He is pleased to use them, are only His instruments. So that all other teachers whatsoever, whether the light of reason, or external directors, or rules prescribed in books, &c., are no further nor otherwise to be followed or hearkened to, than as they are subordinate and conformable to the internal directions and inspirations of God's Holy Spirit, or as God invites, instructs, and moves us to have recourse unto them, by them to be informed in His will, and by Him enabled to perform it; and that if they be made use of any other ways, they will certainly mislead us.

This is by all mystical writers acknowledged so fundamental a truth, that without acknowledging it and working according to it, it is in vain to enter into the exercises of an internal contemplative life. So that to say (as too commonly it is said by authors who pretend to be spiritual, but have no taste of these mystic matters), take all your instructions from without, from external teachers or books, is all one as to say, have nothing at all to do with the ways of contemplation, which can be taught by no other but God, or by those whom God especially instructs and appoints determinately for the disciple's present exigency. So that it is God only that internally teaches both the teacher and disciple, and His inspirations are the only lesson for both. All our light, therefore, is from divine illumination, and all our strength as to these things is from the divine operation of the Holy Ghost on our wills and affections. (1. 2. 1. 5–6)

God's will may be communicated to the soul in two ways: internally and externally. Externally, divine calls may come through books, through a spiritual director, or through the laws of the Church and the precepts of superiors. Baker gives a few preliminary cautions: not to expect internal guidance in trivial matters or in ones under the jurisdiction of superiors; not to make sudden resolutions, or to act while influenced by passions; and, above all, not to expect or desire miraculous intervention or visions.

Baker, like St. John of the Cross[5] and most other mystics, cautions his reader strongly against desiring or too readily accepting the more spectacular effects that sometimes accompany contemplation. St. John of the Cross thought that these effects were often caused by physical weakness; that (when they were not illusory) they were distortions of God's effort to communicate with the soul due to imperfections in the subject and, therefore, nothing to take pride in. The mystics were only too aware how much damage could be done by someone who took these manifestations too seriously, and published them abroad without permission, reflection, or humility. Numerous instances of harm done during the seventeenth century by such uncontrolled or false revelations could be cited by both Protestants and Catholics. The Anabaptists of Muenster, who proclaimed the Millennium and perished in the destruction of their city, are a familiar example of the catastrophes that can occur from spreading private inspirations abroad. The later history of the Jansenists in France, who danced wildly in the graveyards, is a regrettable example among Catholics. Many of the abuses of the English Civil War, such as the libertinism of the Ranters or the murderous righteousness of some sectarian enthusiasts, could be multiplied at length.[6]

The sixteenth and early seventeenth centuries were a time of spiritual ferment and of popular interest in religion, on the Continent as well as in England, and they were, therefore, also one of prophets and false prophets. Baker is more stringent in his treatment of visions than he is about any other spiritual question: "As for extraordinary supernatural inspirations, illuminations, apparitions, voices, conversations with spirits, messages from heaven, &c., a spiritual internal liver is forbidden to pretend to, or so much as desire them; yea, rather to pray against them, lest he should abuse them to vanity and pride; and, moreover, never to admit or esteem them for such, and much less to put in execution anything that seems to be such a way commanded, till they have been first examined, judged, and approved by superiors" (*Sancta Sophia,* 1.2.1.13).

Baker gives several reasons for the necessity of interior guidance by God. One is that only God can fully penetrate the depths of a soul and see what its needs are. The secrets of the soul can be seen only "by Him to whom alone . . . our hearts and all the secret inclinations and motions of them are naked and transparent." This is why St. Benedict concerned himself so much with external details when he formulated his monastic rule: "he contents himself with ordaining prescriptions for the exterior only, because he knew that the interior could only be directed by God." But all the exterior prescriptions of the Rule are designed to best dispose the soul for interior receptiveness to God's guidance (*Sancta Sophia,* 1.2.4.6–7).

The second reason inspiration is needed is that, even in carrying out obvious duties, the will must be purified and the intentions perfected: "God does not reward works (even though good in their own nature) which we do merely out of the impulse of nature . . . and undertake without a Divine call from God." In the *Inner Life,* Baker writes: "The mere cessation of action at the Divine bidding is a thousand times more pleasing to God than the noblest and most wonderful deeds performed out of a mere natural impulse" (191, 238).[7]

Since every soul is different, it is meant to approach God in a different way: only God can know the path that He wants it to follow. Some of these paths may seem strange and eccentric, and the complexity of each person's intended development is beyond the scope of the necessarily simplistic guidance of spiritual writers. Baker has set down his experiences in the *Secretum, sive mysticum* in order to inform his readers

that there be varieties and strange passages in the ways toward God, and that if God shall offer to call or lead them by any such or other unknown way they shall not refuse or forbear to embrace the same, but shall pursue it according to the invitation and enablement they shall have for it from God.

And various, yea infinite, are or may be the ways of God. One may read all the ways that he finds written, but he is to follow that way— and no other—by which God calleth him, whether he have read the same way in books or have not. (*Confessions,* 109)

Even a spiritual director, working with an individual person, unless he himself seeks God's inspiration and effaces his own personality, is likely to force his charge into a conventional and inappropriate mold.

Internal inspiration, Baker writes, is usually received in two ways. One is by a "clearing of the understanding," in which a problem that formerly seemed murky becomes clear to the natural reason by means of supernatural enlightenment. The other is by an impulse in the will, "by which God doth immediately signify His will to the intellective soul in virtue of prayer . . . by imprinting a blind, reasonless motion into the superior will, giving it a weight and propension to one side of the doubt" (*Sancta Sophia*, 1.2.7.9–12). Although one should have a quiet confidence that God will, if properly approached, inspire him to do the right thing, he should not expect Him to intervene obviously: "A soul must not expect an apparent evident certitude, as spiritual writers say; for God, to keep the soul in humility, does not use to give an absolute assurance" (1.2.7.26). Since the fall, because of the decay of his faculties and the loss of direct, conscious contact with God, man is no longer able to receive God's inspirations clearly or to differentiate with certitude between the promptings of God and those of corrupted nature or the devil. For this reason, the active man never has a very clear idea of God's particular will for him, although he may have sufficient grace for salvation. The still, small voice of God (1 Kings, xix:11–13) can be heard only by the contemplative, who has done away with busy distractions; for God's commands are usually drowned out by the world's business.

Baker's directions for removing obstructions to inspiration are, in effect, the same as those that prepare the soul for contemplation. "There are," he writes, "two general impediments that nature lays in our way to hinder us from attending to God. The first is distracting images; the second, unquiet passions." The easiest way to clear the mind of distracting images is to avoid taking them into the mind in the first place; to concentrate one's thoughts on loving God. Baker sums up this process as "abstraction of life." The remedy for unquiet passions is twofold: mortification of all inordinate affections toward creatures, and cultivation of the habit of calm and cheerfulness, "not suffering any passions to be raised in our minds during our imperfect state, no, not although they should be directed upon good and holy objects, because they will obscure and disorder our spirits" (*Sancta Sophia*, 1.2.5.2–3).

Baker writes that whoever prepares himself properly and follows in a humble spirit the guidance of inspiration never goes astray. Baker does not mean that everything such a person does will succeed, for it may be that failure will be better for his soul; indeed, God may even lead someone into an enterprise that he is unable to carry out. Baker gives the example of a hermit, commanded to fast, who falls ill. He prays for guidance as to whether or not he should break his fast, and it seems to him that he should not. As a result, he seriously weakens himself. What has been bad for his body, however, has been good for his soul; and, by obeying God's will as far as it is revealed to him, he has advanced his spiritual state (*Sancta Sophia,* 1.2.4.5).

Although an active man must be guided chiefly by external rules, since he is usually deaf to God's voice, the securest guide for the contemplative is the Holy Spirit, who alone can lead him in the ways that are proper to his individual personality. The more the important events of life take place in the interior of the soul, the more inspiration is needed as a guide: "Most securely, therefore, may we, yea, with all confidence ought we to yield ourselves to be disposed of by God, and to follow Him in any ways that He will lead us, both for the exterior and interior, through light and darkness, through bitter and sweet. And what doubt can there be of erring, having such a guide, which always leads the soul through the paths of mortification and renunciation of self-will? Although sometimes some special ways may to our or others' natural judgments seem strange and perhaps impertinent" (*Sancta Sophia,* 1.2.8.4).

Although Baker stresses interior inspiration in his approach to spirituality, he does not neglect exterior matters. He assumes on the part of his readers a knowledge of doctrines, regular use of the sacraments, and submission to ecclesiastical authority.[8] The interior freedom to follow the dictates of the Holy Spirit must exist within a framework of obedience to external law. And, although the Holy Spirit is the soul's only teacher, Baker assumes that proper use will be made of spiritual books or whatever aids are available. Exterior laws are one form in which divine guidance is embodied and transmitted to the soul: "All laws, therefore, all constitutions, precepts, and commands of superiors, and all external or internal duties of obligation by virtue of our state of life as Christians, or moreover as religious or ecclesiastical persons, &c., are, indeed, and so to be esteemed by us, true divine calls, necessarily to be attended to, known, and performed by us" (*Sancta*

Sophia, 1.2.9.3). The individual can never be at liberty to plead private enlightenment against legitimate external authority.

If, to give an extreme example, God inspires the soul internally to some course and a superior wrongly forbids it, then, although the superior will be held accountable for his action, the soul can profit only by obedience because it is now the will of God. Baker is most insistent on the importance of obedience if there is a conflict between interior and exterior guidance: "Therefore, whatsoever internal suggestions, motions, or impulses we may find that shall be contrary or prejudicial to such external calls to obedience and regularity, we are to be so far from hearkening to them or esteeming them for divine, that we ought to despise and reject them, judging them to be no better than diabolical illusions. Yea, this is to hold, although the said external laws, commands, or observances be such as we in our private judgment cannot think to be very proper or convenient for us in particular" (*Sancta Sophia,* 1.2.9.5).

Even to pray for enlightenment in some matter in which the individual is already guided by an evident rule or command—as if the choice were doubtful—is a "vain, presumptuous, and dangerous tempting of God"; and such conduct deserves to be answered by illusions or the "devil's counterfeiting" (*Sancta Sophia,* 1.2.7.27). The matters proper for interior resolution, in which the soul may legitimately seek for inspiration, are those that "of themselves and in the general are indifferent, but yet which, being well chosen, may and will advance the soul; for in no other things but such can there be any doubt" (1.2.8.8). These matters, although morally indifferent in themselves, can often have momentous moral consequences. To take an example from the life of Baker himself, his decision to leave England for the Continent in 1624, together with his decision to accept the post at Cambray, was morally and rationally neutral; but it was of utmost importance to his spiritual development. The consequences of such decisions cannot be foreseen: they are beyond the scope of reason or of conscience; but, if they are not to be resigned to chance, then they must be guided by divine providence.

Inspiration can, however, concern itself with morally obvious matters as well. Here its role is not so much to guide as to correct and purify motives, to encourage the soul to perform known duties "with perfection and purity of intention, in and for God only, as if He had immediately and visibly imposed them upon us" (*Sancta Sophia,* 1.2.9.4). In the effort to be perfect, interior motives must be perfected; and the soul can accomplish this aim only by means of God's internal guidance and grace. Therefore, although it would be presumptuous to pray for guidance when the right course of action is known, it is legitimate to pray for the grace needed to act with purity of intention, or for help to accept something that is repugnant to one's nature.

III *Inspiration and Spiritual Direction*

Baker's approach to the question of inspiration was important not only because of Catholic defensiveness in the face of doctrines promulgated by the Protestant reformers but also because the Counter Reformation saw the growth of a widespread spirituality that depended on spiritual direction. St. Francis de Sales, as well as St. Ignatius, stressed the importance of the spiritual director. As David Knowles states, "When Father Baker wrote, the directive movement was at its height in Catholic Europe. It was indeed the golden age of the confessor." [9] But spiritual direction is a delicate matter in the case of a contemplative, since his state is hidden: the arena of his spiritual struggle and progress is within the soul; occurrences of importance cannot be accurately put into words; and, if the director is not more advanced and more experienced than his pupil, his advice may do more harm than good.

Baker does not argue that spiritual direction is bad or unnecessary for the contemplative. He recognized that the lack of "a better and more expert master" led to his giving up prayer after attaining "passive contemplation" at Cook Hill. Otherwise, "he had not so fallen, but had prosecuted and held on his course." Similarly, in the absence of a qualified confessor, he was in error not to have studied more spiritual books; his reading "did not suffice to instruct him for the various passages that do occur . . . in a spiritual life" (*Confessions,* 78, 81–82).

While Baker admitted that a confessor was usually necessary, however, he felt that the need occurred mainly at the beginning. In fact, the chief business of a spiritual director is to teach the soul "how to dispose herself to hearken to and follow God's internal teaching, and to stand in no more need of consulting her external director." Like that of his modern counterpart, the psychoanalyst, the confessor's duty is to avoid impressing his own ideas or personality on his charge; he is to assist him to follow his own proper course: "He is only God's usher, and must lead souls in God's way and not his own" (*Sancta Sophia*, 1.2.2.2–3, 27).

In the *Inner Life of Dame Gertrude More*, Baker, who was Dame Gertrude's director, devotes a great deal of attention to this theme of self-effacement. The director should avoid personal friendship with his charges and be wary of any human bond that might interfere with the growing ties between them and God:

Indeed, the office of director is not to teach a particular method to the disciple, but to give general instructions by which the soul may get into her interior, and when she has once got there, to observe the Divine admonitions and guidance, instead of following the methods of books, or opinions of others, custom, or what at other times had proved profitable. This point is of such moment for God's honour and the good of souls that I think a better deed could not be done than to proclaim this doctrine all through God's Church by the pen of some spiritual man who can express himself clearly and skilfully. (145–46)

This approach applies, naturally, only to those who have the "propensity" for an interior life; but these, Baker writes, are many (*Inner Life*, 73–74).

The aim of the confessor should be to set souls free, to give them liberty to follow their own proper courses. It is, however, impossible for the Christian to conceive of an absolute freedom and independence because the individual must always be dependent on God for his existence. The issue is not, therefore, between dependence and independence; it is between dependence on man and his formulas or dependence on God and the guidance of His Spirit.[10] A commonplace of Christian doctrine is that the service of God is, in the words of the Book of Common Prayer, "perfect freedom." As St. Augustine writes: "Only he is free in service who gladly does the will of his Lord. And consequently he who is the servant of sin is free only for sinning. Wherefore he cannot be free to act righteously unless he is made free from sin and has begun to be a servant of righteousness. This is the true liberty, because of joy for the upright act; and no less is it pious servitude, because of obedience to the commandment." [11]

Baker suggests not only that a slavish obedience to spiritual books or directors be avoided but that the would-be contemplative must also avoid enslavement to his own whims. It is common for a beginner to make vows that he is unable to keep, to assume voluntary mortifications that will crush his enthusiasm, or to set himself a course that his constitution will not allow. Therefore the beginner must avoid slavery to his own zeal; for willfulness, even when well-intentioned, can destroy true freedom of the will. "Liberty of spirit," Baker writes, "is freedom of spirit to attend to and follow the light of the Holy Spirit. Opposed to liberty of spirit are human notions imposed on the soul out of her own head" (*Inner Life,* 211). Since human nature cannot be depended on, the soul must rely on God to direct it in the ways that are best for it; for, unlike God, the soul is incapable of seeing where the roots of its faults lie, or how its potential personality is best to be developed and set free from the limitations of original sin. Self-knowledge can only be achieved by first approaching God and submitting oneself to Him. Baker quotes St. Augustine: "If I should know Thee, I should know myself" (*Inner Life,* 223).

That a confessor, by arbitrary directions and limitations, could do great damage to the soul in his care was not a new idea. St. John of the Cross often expresses a similar view; he even writes that anyone who hinders a soul from contemplation does a worse deed "than the disquieting and ruining of many souls of a more ordinary nature which have not attained to this state of such supreme fineness and delicacy. It is as though a portrait of supreme beauty were touched by a clumsy hand, and were daubed with strange, crude colours. This would be a greater and a more crying shame than if many more ordinary portraits were besmeared in this way, and a matter of greater grief and pity." [12]

Baker follows his own advice: he frequently remarks that his doctrines and methods are to be followed only as closely and as far as may be proper for the individual reader. Nor does he attempt to guide the reader in the higher stages of prayer. He suggests ways in which the soul may prepare itself for the contemplative life, but he does not presume to give directions for what must depend on God's grace and guidance: "A soul that is come to this state is above all instructors and instructions, a divine light being her guide in all manner of things." In the higher ranges of contemplation, interior inspiration predominates; and, as God and not the soul becomes increasingly the agent, it becomes all-important. Echoing St. Paul, Baker says of the contemplative soul that, "in a word, it is not she that now lives, but Christ and His Holy Spirit that lives, reigns, and operates in her" (*Sancta Sophia,* 3.2.1.14). This state, therefore, Baker seldom touches on.

Although God's inspiration rarely comes to the beginner as an obvious or even a perceptible effect, nevertheless it can infallibly be relied on to bring about whatever is best for the soul's advancement. Baker is confident "that if all spiritual books in the world were lost, and there were no external directors at all," a soul with a natural aptness and an elementary instruction in the Catholic faith could, with perseverance and reliance on God's guidance, "walk clearly in perfect light, and with all possible security, and would not fail in due time to arrive at perfect contemplation" (*Sancta Sophia,* 1.2.3.17). Since spiritual books *are* available and since superiors exist and competent directors are often to be found, they should be properly used; and not to use them would be to tempt God. Nevertheless, in the absence of these aids, the soul can be entirely confident that God will provide all requisite guidance directly.

IV *Inspiration and Conversion*

We saw in Chapter 2 that Baker applied his conception of personal inspiration to conversion. He believed that converts could best be made not by argument but by inducing them to pray with an open mind for guidance. In an age of controversy this approach was infrequent. Part of the reason for the success of Baker's approach to conversion is suggested by another moderate, the Presbyterian Richard Baxter: "In controversy, it is fierce opposition which is the bellows to kindle a resisting zeal; when, if they be neglected and their opinions lie a while despised, they usually cool and come again to themselves." Baxter also says that "in a learning way men are ready to receive the truth, but in a disputing way they come armed against it with prejudice and animosity." [13] Baxter arrived at this opinion by bitter experience in the religious disputes of the Civil-War period.

Evidently, however, something more is needed to convert people than simply not arguing, whether it be good example, charismatic persuasiveness, or the aid of divine inspiration. In any event, Baker's conversion of others shows that he really believed in the spiritual freedom and personal inspiration that come to those who devoutly seek them in prayer. Therefore, in *Sancta So-*

phia Baker writes that superiors ought to send contemplatives or spiritual monks on the missions, rather than those who are active and disputative; and what he writes about the ideal missionary might well be applied to Baker himself: "Moreover, in latter times, experience hath witnessed that some humble and devout, though not so learned, missioners have prospered better in converting souls than the most acute and cunning controvertists, and have by their humility, modesty, and edifying conversation, but especially by the practice and teaching of internal prayer, gained to Catholic unity those souls that many other, most skilful in disputes, and withal enabled with experience, have for long time in vain attempted" (1.3.10.9). Baker was not unlearned, but it was certainly characteristic of him never to take pride in his education and never to engage in controversy or dispute with potential converts.

V *Personal and Institutional Religion*

The attitude of the more enthusiastic sects in the seventeenth century toward inspiration is well known; Richard Hooker remarks: "When they and their Bibles were alone together, what strange fantastical opinion soever at any time entered into their heads, their use was to think the Spirit taught it them." So at least it appeared to a conservative churchman, and even the visionary George Fox remarked that the Ranters and Seekers ran to extremes.[14]

According to Fr. Philip Hughes, "the basic principle of the sixteenth-century Reformers had been the right of private judgement. They refused to acknowledge . . . an impersonal teaching authority in religious matters. With the Bible at his disposal every man would come surely and safely to a knowledge of divine truth." [15] But, although many of the English Puritans and sectaries continued to stress private judgment, the more conservative Protestant Churches abandoned it in practice. Hierarchies and rubrics were retained; the clergy were licensed and required to subscribe to certain definite practices and doctrines; and interpretation of the Bible was still taught to future ministers at Oxford and at Cambridge, while differing interpretations were frowned on. According to Fr. Ronald Knox, the trend in the major Protestant churches from private judgment back to institutionalism began as early as the occasion on which Luther turned his back on Munzer at Wittenberg.[16]

Luther's conception of salvation by faith, which is attainable only by means of God's grace, implies that inward enlightenment is important. Likewise, Calvin's doctrine of election leads to a strong concern for the personal relationship between the individual soul and God, which no interposition of hierarchy or intercessor can interfere with. But Luther's approach to these matters proved more theoretical than actual, and the Lutheran Church retained hierarchy, ritual, and authority; Calvin's approach was even more authoritarian, so that, as Milton to his sorrow was to learn, many of his spiritual descendants became new forcers of conscience.

Indeed, the Quakers were the only sect in England that stressed inspiration and inward enlightenment in practice as well as in theory that long survived; the rest died out, lost their members to the Quakers,[17] or went underground, to be given new expression by Wesley in the following century. We have a glimpse of these undercurrents in John Bunyan's *Grace Abounding to the Chief of Sinners* and in the records of the temporarily more successful Puritans in New England.

The problem was how a group of men believing in a personal religion and in personal interpretation of Scripture could long remain a group in any real sense of the word, with no fixed structure to hold the members together. Often, leadership depended on the popularity or the holiness of individual men; the person was respected rather than the office; and, when he died, the continuance of the sect was endangered. In other cases, authority might be vested in a group of elders, or in all the full members; but in the course of time the elders died, and the younger generations never experienced the expected regeneration of soul or infusion of inner light. Such, indeed, was the tragic experience of the settlers of Massachusetts. One of the main forces holding such groups together in England was the opposition of the Established Church, so that many referred to themselves only as Dissenters. Dissent, however, is a negative quality and makes a poor binding force.

The sects in the early seventeenth century had yet to face these problems, however. Many of the passages in Fox's journal show his thirst for a personal, inward religion. His flight from hierarchy and authority illustrates the desire of many of his less articulate contemporaries for a living, charismatic faith. When Cressy remarks that the Catholic Church should assume a reasonable position on the subject of inspiration, he recognizes the desires of all those seeking, like Fox, a closer relation with God. The failure to retain or provide an inner spirituality in the mass of its people cost Catholicism greatly at the Reformation. Fox thus tells the story of his journey from organized religion to inner faith:

Now after I had received that opening from the Lord that to be bred at Oxford or Cambridge was not sufficient to fit a man to be a minister of Christ, I regarded the priests less, and looked more after the Dissenting people. Among them I saw there was some tenderness; and many of them came afterwards to be convinced, for they had some openings. But as I had forsaken the priests, so I left the Separate preachers also, and those called the most experienced people; for I saw there was none among them all that could speak to my condition. And when all my hopes in them and in all men were gone, so that I had nothing outwardly to help me, nor could I tell what to do; then, oh! then I heard a voice which said, "There is one, even Christ Jesus, that can speak to thy condition"; and when I heard it, my heart did leap for joy. Then the Lord did let me see why there was none upon the earth that could speak to my condition, namely, that I might give Him all the glory; for all are concluded under sin, and shut up in unbelief, as I had been, that Jesus Christ might have the pre-eminence, who enlightens, and gives grace and faith and power. Thus when God doth work, who shall let it? and this I knew experimentally. My desires after the Lord grew stronger, and zeal in the pure knowledge of God, and of Christ alone, without the help of any man, book, or writing. For though I read the Scriptures that spake of Christ and of God, yet I knew Him not, but by revelation, as He who hath the key did open, and as the Father of Life drew me to His Son by His Spirit.[18]

Although, unlike Baker, Fox dismisses all outward law or authority, there are nevertheless noticeable similarities between the two men. When Fox writes that none but the Lord can speak to his "condition," he parallels Baker's insistence that every soul is different and that only God knows the soul's needs. Fox's "tenderness"—a favorite word with him—has some of the same implications as Baker's "propensity": his "openings" are Baker's "divine calls." Above all, these two men are alike in their desire for an experiential knowledge of God. There was a great desire in Prot-

estant and Catholic alike for the kind of religious freedom that
Baker advocated and for the personal approach to God that he
taught.

The differences in attitude toward inspiration of Quaker and
Catholic mystic are perhaps greater than the similarities. Baker's
conception of inspiration through authority or outward necessity
has no counterpart in Fox's beliefs. Baker advocated keeping all
revelations from God strictly private, at least until they had the
approval of superiors, but the Quakers at this time published
them abroad. Baker believed that the road to perfection was long
and difficult, finding its ultimate consummation in death; the
Quakers in theory believed in a much earlier perfection. Fr. Knox
says: "Our traditional doctrine is that grace perfects nature . . .
but leaves it nature still. The assumption of the enthusiast is
bolder and simpler; for him, grace has destroyed nature, and replaced it." [19] This belief in perfection did not, of course, survive
very long without setbacks; but Fox himself held it. He writes that
not only can man reach "Adam's perfection," but he can surpass it
in this life and "grow up to the measure of the stature of the fulness of Christ." [20] This extreme confidence is dangerous and can
easily be perverted to antinomianism—the conviction that one is
perfect and therefore by definition nothing one does can be wrong.

Learning, particularly as it was instilled at Oxford and Cambridge, was often attacked by Puritan or by Quaker, although on
the whole Puritans respected education. Wycliffe, a Balliol man,
had asserted that "a single unlettered preacher does more, by
God's grace, for the profit of the Church than a whole number of
classmen." [21] The reasoning behind this statement is that it is not
vain learning but God's inspiration that makes a true minister.
Therefore, the attitude is not so much rooted in anti-intellectualism as in a strong feeling that for a preacher the inspiration of
God is paramount. The enthusiasm for an inspired clergy did,
however, often manifest itself in anti-intellectual statements; and
the idea of inspiration was much abused. Baxter, like many of the
Catholics, distrusted inspiration for a while because of the excesses he witnessed: "I more sensibly perceive that the Spirit is
the great witness of Christ and Christianity to the world. And
though the folly of fanatics tempted me long to overlook the
strength of this testimony of the Spirit, while they placed it in a
certain internal assertion or enthusiastic inspiration, yet now I see

that the Holy Ghost in another manner is the witness of Christ
and his agent in the world." [22] Catholics and apologists for the
Established Church were not the only ones who saw danger in too
strong an emphasis on inspiration and who were thereby forced
into undesirable positions on the subject.

The more extreme sects—Anabaptists, Behmenists, Seekers,
Ranters—made divine inspiration a cornerstone of their belief;
and they sometimes denied the authority of Scripture as well as
that of ecclesiastical hierarchies. They stressed the gospel in the
heart or the presence of Christ in the soul; without this light, the
Scriptures were only so many words. The old man, in St. Paul's
phrase, was dead; and Christ lived in His elect. Great emphasis
was put on regeneration, on what came to be called "seeing the
light." Wheat and tares were no longer to grow up together in the
new churches because only those who walked in the light were
permitted full membership. A favorite text was that the letter kill-
eth, but the spirit giveth life. The letter, of course, had ruled the
Church of Rome as well as the pre-Christian Jews; and it seemed
to many that it also ruled the Church of England.

The Church of England took a defensive position against private inspiration. Enthusiasm quickly became a pejorative word,
and in the balance between institutional and personal religion
there were actually some areas in which Roman Catholic orthodoxy allowed more freedom than Anglicanism. Because the institutional base and the theological structure of the Established
Church were more recent than the Catholic ones and because
there was no official machinery for distinguishing between accept-
able forms of mysticism or private inspiration and those poten-
tially harmful to the balance established by Elizabeth, the leaders
of the English Church could permit less experimentation in some
areas than Catholicism could.

Jeremy Taylor, representative of moderate thinking among Anglicans, and concerned more with devotion than polemic, shows a
better than average understanding of what mysticism is, but he
then dismisses it: "There is a degree of meditation so exalted that
it changes the very name, and is called contemplation; and it is
the unitive way of religion, that is, it consists in unions and adher-
ences to God." But, he goes on: "It is more healthful and nutritive
to dig the earth, and to eat of her fruits, than to stare upon the
greatest glories of the heavens: So unsatisfying a thing is rapture

and transportation to the soul; it often distracts the faculties, but seldom does advantage piety, and is full of danger in the greatest of its lustre." [23]

Helen White suggests that one reason for the low reputation of mysticism in England was the dissolution of the monasteries: "Just as the cult of the saints, of which the saint's life had been the literary expression, had been the foundation of the whole system of shrines and offerings and pilgrimages against which the Reformers inveighed, so the book of contemplation was the literary expression of that type of religious activity which found its institutional embodiment in the monasteries." [24] Although contemplation is possible outside the monastery or the hermit's retreat, it is rare. The official government position for a long time was that contemplation was a cloak for doing nothing or worse, for abusing the people who had endowed the monasteries. Only by attacking the practices of the monks could the seizure of monastic property be justified. It is significant that Henry VIII felt it necessary to treat the Carthusians with the utmost ruthlessness; their contemplative unworldliness actually counted against them.[25] The dislike of monks that many Protestants already felt was encouraged by the government and its supporters. As a result, the ideal of contemplation suffered, even in the opinion of men whose attitude toward personal religion and inspiration might have led them to respect it.

Although we may think of the religious situation in the seventeenth century as a broad spectrum in which the dissenting churches were on the left, the Church of England in the middle, and Catholicism on the right, it was also common at that time to say that true religion, or the Church of England, was a mean between atheism or skepticism on the left and superstition on the right.[26] In this scheme, Quakers and Catholics were both on the right. To a moderate member of the Church of England Augustine Baker and Robert Barclay appeared to share certain attitudes that the Church of England disparaged. Charles Dodd (a Catholic) said of Baker in 1742 that "in some of his notions he seem'd to chime with the Quakers." [27] Quaker and Catholic mystic alike valued a personal and direct approach to God, and both tried to respect divine inspiration in practice as well as in theory.

Fr. Ronald Knox, in his study of enthusiasm, writes that through the ages there has been a constant "conflict between the char-

ismatic and the institutional." Rufus Jones, who notes that the
proponents of a charismatic religion have often been mystics, then
says:

To the bearers of it [spiritual religion], the historic Church, with its
crystallized system and its vast machinery, always seemed "unspiritual"
and traditional. They believed, each time the movement appeared, that
they had found the way to more abundant life, that the Spirit had
come upon them inaugurating a higher order of Christianity, and they
always felt that their religion of direct experience, of invading energy,
of inspirational insights, of charismatic bestowals, and of profound
emotional fervour was distinctly "spiritual," as contrasted with the
historic Church, which claimed indeed a divine origin and divine
"deposits," but which, they believed, lacked the continuous and progressive leadership of the Spirit.

Herschel Baker speaks of "the antithesis between an inward,
searching, and intensely subjective as opposed to an outward, formal, and communal quality of religious emotion." This antithesis,
he goes on to say, is *"au fond,* the antithesis between Puritan and
Anglican; and . . . it had portentous consequences not only for
Church discipline, but even for political theory." [28]
  In Protestantism, the conflict between personal and institutional
religion was open. Most Puritans wanted to do away as far as
possible with the outward framework of ritual, dogma, and authority. Orthodox Catholic mystics like Augustine Baker, however,
sought to preserve both elements, inward and outward, in a har-
monious union. Therefore, in emphasizing the importance of spiritual freedom, Baker never pleads for releasing the bonds of obedience to superiors; instead, he asks that superiors respect the
freedom of the soul and govern their commands by the enlightenment they themselves receive. Inspiration, instead of doing
away with hierarchy, should enlighten it from top to bottom,
should guide the actions of those in authority, and free their commands from arbitrary rigidity or harshness.
  Baker thus takes a middle position between the demands of
the charismatic and the institutional. Because the Catholic Church
and the Benedictine Order of his time seemed to him to stress the
institutional at the expense of the spiritual, he emphasizes freedom, inspiration, and inward religion; but he never loses sight of
his ideal of freedom within a framework of order—a goal, indeed,

which he shared with many moderate Protestants. Like Milton, Baker's younger contemporary, he was not a man to be frightened by the proliferation of sects or by the danger that freedom might pose to orthodoxy; like Cressy, he believed that to deny the doctrine of inspiration would be to "betray the Christian religion."

CHAPTER 6

The Via Media *and Mortification*

I *The* Via Media

IT IS a remarkable characteristic of most of the great mystics that, although their goal is unlimited and they set no bounds to their desire to approach nearer and nearer to God, they preserve a prudential moderation and considerable common sense. St. Teresa's practicality is proverbial; it is repeatedly evident in her writings. The great monastic reforms and the new foundations were accomplished not only because of the spiritual vitality of the founders but also because of their grasp of necessary detail. Thus, for example, St. Vincent de Paul, who was at the center of the spiritual revival in seventeenth-century France, wrote some thirty to fifty thousand letters to keep his reforms moving.[1] Similarly, St. Ignatius spent his last eighteen years at a desk in Rome,[2] and St. Bernard corresponded with people all over Europe. According to Bremond: "It is mysticism which has given us our greatest men of action."[3]

Baker also combines, in his own way, the elements of unlimited spiritual goals with common sense in attaining them. He is one of the most reliable guides for beginners in the mystical way, because he presents his doctrines in sober, discursive, carefully qualified form, making no attempt to sway the reader's emotions. Some mystical treatises are dangerous for the uncritical reader who may be aroused to enthusiasm by accounts of visions, ecstasies, or the heights of mysticism, without realizing what austerities must first be passed through. Baker, however, treats every aspect of the preliminary stages in the clearest possible fashion.

According to Watkin, "Fr. Baker's spiritual doctrine is the most practically valuable that I am acquainted with." As Baker continually reminds us, moderation never compromises with respect to the goal, which must be sought in spite of any obstacle whatever. But the goal must be reached by a prudent understanding of human nature, particularly in the beginning, and by patiently

waiting for God's own time. "In this moderation, this consideration for human weakness, which nevertheless is never false to the
. . . principles which determine man's union with God," Baker
embodies the discretion characteristic of the Benedictine Rule.[4]

Love of moderation was Baker's reason for joining the Benedictines; he held this ideal from the first. It is Baker's great virtue
that mystical vision does not destroy his sense of the practical instruction needed by the uninitiated, to whom he especially directed his work. He believed that many more people were capable
of contemplation than actually practiced it. Even more than meditation, contemplation was within the reach of the unlearned. Although a more advanced form of prayer, contemplation requires
less learning or intellect, more courage and resolution.

One of the perversions of contemplative prayer is Quietism,
which Fr. Knox calls "a morbid growth on the healthy body of
mysticism." [5] The Quietists taught an absolute passivity of soul in
prayer, demanding complete indifference even to the question of
whether or not the soul would be saved. The Quietist movement
had its roots among the *Alumbrados* or Illuminists of sixteenth-
century Spain, appeared in Rome early in the seventeenth century, and spread to France, where Fénelon was influenced by it.
Two of Baker's sources, the *Life of the Spirit Approved* by de
Rojas and Benet Canfield's *Rule of Perfection*, were placed on
the Index in the latter part of the century. Neither author was
actually a Quietist, but each was apparently guilty of ambiguity
or of incautious hyperbole in a few passages.

Baker does not imitate their use of extravagant terms. In a passage in the *Commentary* he writes: "Father Benet Fitch [Can-
field] calleth this abstraction by the name of *annihilation*. But the
term of *annihilation* doth not please me so well, and is not so free
from error, as are the terms of *abstraction, transcending, sur-
mounting,* and *forgetting* of one's self and all creatures. And our
author of the *Cloud* terms it a *keeping under the cloud of forgetting*" (182).

St. John of the Cross occasionally speaks of annihilation of the
soul in God, but carefully and rarely. The distinction in terminology is not important now, since Quietism is no longer in vogue;
but careless use of terms with a subject as difficult to discuss as
mysticism is not helpful. Although Baker faced considerable opposition before 1657 on account of his doctrine of inspiration, he

was never seriously suspected of Quietist tendencies. He was accused of verging on illuminism by Fr. Hull, but the charge had no grounds and went no further. In 1655, Fr. Claude White tried to get the Abbess of Cambray to surrender Baker's manuscripts for inspection and editing—an incident discussed below in Chapter 7—but his exact reasons are unknown.

II *Inspiration and the* Via Media

Inspiration, or the pretence of inspiration, is often a sign of extremism or of religious enthusiasm. Although it is central to Baker's kind of spirituality, it does not take the exaggerated forms found in some sects. According to Baker, inspiration not only works in harmony with law and obedience, but when there is a choice between following inspiration or human inclination, inspiration is often more moderate. If someone tried to prepare himself for contemplation without guidance, he would probably resort to austerities or prolonged periods of prayer that would quickly weary and disable his soul. Since only God can fully understand the state of the soul and its needs, the inspirations He sends are less arbitrary and do less violence to nature than the advice of man.

The moderation of divine guidance is illustrated by Baker's description of the spiritual development of his disciple, Dame Gertrude More in the *Inner Life:* "She says that she was to amend her life as she could, and not as she would; that it was God's will that she should await a longer time for total amendment; that in the meantime she should exercise patience with herself, amending little by little, and as she could, and that if she had proceeded otherwise she would never have corrected anything at all" (110).

One must reform himself slowly, with moderation, in accordance with God's will; because, if the natural desires are thwarted all at once, no good will result. "The Holy Spirit, indeed, dealt with Dame Gertrude as with all souls. He accommodates His grace to their natural disposition . . . [and] ever seeks to reform little by little what in it is a hindrance to profound introversion and perfection. He does not change the natural character, but restrains, subdues the inordinate movements of natural passions and desires" (*Inner Life,* 94).

This is one more reason why inspiration is necessary for an interior life—because only God can see which actions are needed and which must be postponed; which faults must be repaired and which must wait. "Everyone is to observe the grace and ability bestowed on him by God and to act accordingly, and neither more nor less. He is not to do more, lest he harm and destroy the body, and so utterly disable himself from doing as much as he might otherwise have done. He is not to do less, because he would then neglect the grace given him or offered him by God, and thereby incur blame or sin" (*Commentary*, 190).

The reconciliation of the Aristotelian ideal of the mean with the unlimited goal of mysticism, which at first might seem impossible, is accomplished by preserving the mean with regard to methods but by making no compromise in the goal. As the passage quoted from Fr. Knox's *Enthusiasm* in Chapter 5 suggests, the orthodox Christian approach to the question of perfection is that grace does not destroy nature but gradually perfects it.[6] Therefore, though the eventual goal may be as high as union with God, nevertheless discretion must still be exercised in attaining it. In a passage from the *Commentary*, Baker makes it clear that discretion is made possible by following God's inspiration:

Discretion is to be used in regard to . . . all our outward doings, by holding a mean and taking or doing neither too much nor too little. . . . It is best acquired, not by reflecting on those things themselves with solicitude to hold a mean in them, but by tending towards God in the exercise of love. And then will God impart to the soul fitting discretion for those external actions. This discretion . . . is best had and practised in those external things *by a recklessness about them* —that is, by not loving them or affecting them. . . . A man should neglect them and love only God . . . taking those external things as it were in his way . . . that he may be able to hold on in his journey, and not for any love he beareth to those things themselves. (206)

Thus we have yet another paradox: moderation in worldly things is best preserved by unworldliness, and discretion by "recklessness"; high ends are best achieved by keeping to a mean, and this mean in turn is preserved by following what is usually a favorite doctrine of extremists—personal inspiration.

III *Mortification*

In the course of this study all the main points of Baker's teachings have been touched on but one: mortification. It has been reserved for discussion here because Baker's treatment of it illustrates his moderation and discretion. Since the Second Treatise of *Sancta Sophia*, on mortification, is clear and logical, it suffices to discuss the subject briefly, mainly with reference to moderation; the reader desiring more detailed knowledge should turn to *Sancta Sophia*. The importance that Baker assigns to mortification is shown by his autobiographical comment that his illness and suffering at Cook Hill enabled him to reach in sixteen months a state of abstraction that he could not afterward attain in sixteen years (*Confessions*, 58). This sickness was not a voluntary mortification but was suffered of necessity; what was voluntary was how he suffered it. As we shall see, Baker believed that voluntary mortifications were generally to be avoided.

Watkin in his study of mysticism compares the contemplative way to purgatory, suggesting that contemplatives suffer in life what others suffer after death. Mystics may be said metaphorically to climb "the mount of purgatory." [7] Indeed, the mystics often compare contemplation to climbing a mountain, as in the title of St. John's work, *The Ascent of Mount Carmel*. The mystic way and purgatory are similar, for in both the soul must be purged of affections for creatures, so it may love God. Baker describes spiritual desolation as the "*Purgatory of Love* in this life" (*Commentary*, 176). Aside from any specific suffering that God may send the contemplative, such as illness, the very process of removing the affections from creatures and from self is painful to fallen nature.

The contemplative way, then, has both positive and negative aspects: positive, because the soul approaches God; negative, because it must give up all other things. These two aspects correspond to the two main elements in the contemplative life: prayer and mortification. "The spiritual life," Baker writes, "consists of these two things—prayer and mortification, the one being insufficient without the other." [8] And a twofold activity is involved in spiritual progress: "We must renounce and fly from ourselves, that we may draw near unto God; we must destroy self-love in our souls, that so the Divine love may be raised and increased in them. Now, it is by Mortification that self-love and all other our natural deordinations, which hinder a divine union, are removed; and it is by Prayer that we directly tend to a divine union" (*Sancta Sophia*, 2.1.2.3).

"All good is comprehended" in these two duties; without them, contemplation is impossible: "Mortification without prayer will be but superficial, or, it is to be feared, hypocritical; and prayer, with a neglect of mortification, will be heartless, distracted, and of small virtue" (*Sancta Sophia*, 2.1.1.5,9). Although prayer and mortification are opposed, one positive and one negative, this distinction is partly artificial: it is necessary if spiritual matters are to be treated discursively, but it is not really present in the higher realms of mysticism. "Prayer is withal in itself the most excellent and effectual mortification; for in and by it the most secret risings of inordinate passions are contradicted, yea, the mind and superior will are wholly abstracted and elevated above nature, so that for the time all passions are quieted, and all creatures, especially ourselves, transcended, forgotten, and in a sort annihilated." In addition, the positive exercise of any virtue is a mortification because in man's fallen state every virtue contradicts some desire of nature, "so that to attain to perfect mortification is to be possessed of all virtues" (*Sancta Sophia*, 2.1.3.8).

Just as the subjects of divine inspirations are not those obvious duties in which the soul requires no enlightenment, the objects of mortification are not obvious sins, but "imperfections; being such sins as, considering the frailty of our nature, can hardly be avoided, and never totally rooted out" (*Sancta Sophia*, 2.1.2.2). One such imperfection is the improper use of lawful things, or impurity of motives in a virtuous act. It is not to be expected in this life that even those who have attained "perfection" will be entirely free of all faults. Perhaps, therefore, Baker's use of the term is questionable, though it has traditionally been used in this sense; it should be understood to mean such perfection as an individual is capable of attaining before death. Baker's meaning is clear in the following passage from *Sancta Sophia:*

If it were required to perfection in a contemplative life that a soul should be entirely free from venial defects, it would be impossible to attain unto it, considering the incurable frailty of our nature, the frequency of temptations, and the incapacity which is in a soul to be in a continual actual guard over herself. . . .

Venial sins, therefore, are not inconsistent with perfection, although they should be committed never so oft out of frailty, subreption, or ignorance. But if they be committed deliberately, advisedly, customarily, and with affection, they render the soul in an incapacity of attaining to perfection in prayer. (2.1.2.11–12)

Thus, although a stubborn and voluntary persistence in the smallest fault is contrary to perfection, human weakness is not. This doctrine is consistent with Baker's belief that the soul must adhere with great perseverance to the guidance of the Holy Spirit, but it need not worry about those imperfections which it is not yet time to correct.

Mortification consists in doing all things enjoined by divine or human law, or by inspiration: in refraining from all things forbidden by these laws; and in patiently bearing all crosses, interior or exterior, whether directly from God or through his creatures. These duties are summarized in the words "to do, or forbear, or suffer, according to her obligations or necessities" (*Inner Life*, 77). The treatise on mortification goes into further details and divisions: general mortification consists of abstraction of life, solitude, silence, and tranquillity of mind. Specific mortifications, discussed in the second part of the treatise, include moderation in eating, combating scrupulosity, practice of humility and obedience, and so on. Baker's advice is always tempered by moderation; he writes with some humor, for example, that it cannot be expected that women will adhere to the rule of silence as fully as men since "among women there can scarce be any recreation if the tongue be too much stinted" (*Sancta Sophia*, 2.1.2.17).

The mortification of the contemplative is different from that of the active man, even in its first stages. Baker advises the contemplative that, instead of struggling against his imperfections, he is to turn away from them and rise above them. Active people "endeavor to mortify their inordinate affections by combatting them purposely and directly, to wit, by meditating discursively on the motives afforded by Christian doctrine to oppose them. . . . Whereas contemplative souls do indirectly, yet far more efficaciously, mortify their passions by transcending them, that is, by elevating and uniting their spirit to God" (*Sancta Sophia*, 2.1.4.8).

In the later stages of the contemplative way, mortification chiefly assumes the form of spiritual suffering in what St. John of the Cross calls "the dark nights." Baker fell away from prayer after his second conversion on account of his ignorance of this stage in the way: a "great and . . . deplorable" misery, an "anguish and desertion," in which the presence of God seems to have disappeared entirely, and the soul is completely unable to pray.

Actually, God remains "in the centre of the spirit beyond all her faculties," but withdraws all consolations and is imperceptible. This "last and of all other greatest trial" prepares the soul for union with God (*Sancta Sophia*, 3.4.5.2,1,8,3). Baker calls it "the great desolation," a term he is credited with originating.[9] The doctrine is not new, for the experience of desolation is common to mystics. In the absence of more information, it is rash to decide which of St. John's "nights" Baker's desolation at Cook Hill corresponded to, if any; but, in spite of some recent disagreement,[10] Baker's seems to have been a genuine mystical desolation.

The most important of the distinctions which Baker makes between various kinds of mortifications is that between necessary and voluntary mortification. Necessary mortifications include unavoidable natural afflictions, such as illness or death; duties proper to one's state of life; directions of spiritual advisers; "works that true discretion requires of us"; evils suffered from other people; and, finally, things commanded "by virtue of an interior divine impulse, with the approbation of our spiritual father." Voluntary mortifications, on the other hand, "are such as on our own heads, and without the advice and judgment of those that are acquainted with our interior, we voluntarily assume or impose on ourselves" (*Sancta Sophia*, 2.1.5.1–3). All such voluntary mortifications are to be avoided, and the spiritual director likewise should not impose them on his charges.[11] In keeping with Baker's doctrine of spiritual freedom, the soul is to avoid entangling itself in arbitrary duties; if the beginner is rash or immoderate in imposing penances on himself, his health or his spirit will suffer, and his advancement will be impossible.

Just as God, through his inspirations, reveals exactly what course the soul should follow, so does he reveal what mortifications are needed. The necessary and unavoidable sufferings that come to an individual are those that God deems necessary. But, unless these sufferings are properly received, they will be valueless. Without grace, they may make a person more "judicious, prudent, and temperate"; but they "pierce not to the spirit itself, to cause any purity therein, or really to diminish self-love" (*Sancta Sophia*, 2.4.1.6). Therefore, as we have seen, mortification and prayer are inseparable; and an interior purity of intention must develop with the acceptance of suffering.

In Baker's insistence that voluntary mortifications must not be

assumed unless under the guidance of inspiration (when they are
no longer voluntary), he is, as usual, not an innovator. Although
throughout history the penitential instinct has become excessive,
most orthodox ascetics have taught what Baker does. He calls it
"folly and inexcusable pride" for souls not well advanced in prayer
to assume voluntary mortifications. "If they be unable to encoun-
ter difficulties which are ordinary and necessary," he asks, "why
should they think themselves prepared for extraordinary ones?"
(*Sancta Sophia*, 2.1.5.12). Some Continental commentators, however, do not agree that Baker's position is that of the great mystics;
for Dom Philibert Schmitz writes: "His attitude of soul with respect to mortification is not that generally taken by the immense
majority of mystics, for whom voluntary suffering becomes a sort
of inward necessity, from a spontaneous élan, irresistible, born of
love and destined to grow. Dom Baker, on the contrary, always
has a dislike for the practice of mortification, for himself and in
his advice to others. . . . Baker's doctrine on this point is invari-
able. He nourished, in reality, a great indulgence of nature." [12]

This criticism may be partly based on differences between
French and English approaches to asceticism; but it is also due to
a misunderstanding of Baker's term "necessary mortification,"
which would certainly include impulses "of inward necessity (de
nécessité intime) . . . irresistible, born of love"; for this kind of
impulse would be the result not of self-will but of divine inspiration. Abbot Cuthbert Butler presents a convincing case for the
orthodoxy of Baker's doctrine within the Benedictine tradition;
and E. I. Watkin writes that, on this point, Baker is "a safer guide,
I venture to think, than the greater continental mystics." [13] As for
the charge that Baker indulges nature, his doctrine is uncompro-
mising with respect to the final goal of mysticism and the essen-
tials of religion; but it is eminently sensible in its assumption that
nature is gradually amended, not annihilated, by grace.

Baker proposes to reach an unlimited goal by the judicious use
of moderation and common sense. For, although mysticism may
seem unreal or visionary to the common man, it is a practical matter for the mystic himself; and, like any other enterprise, it demands prudence, not rashness. Because of the nature of the contemplative way, prudence necessitates an increasing dependence
on the guidance and aid of God, a growing conformity with His

will rather than the use of human reason; but reason must be gradually supplemented and directed by divine inspiration, not replaced by zealous willfulness. Like almost all the great contemplative writers, Baker was an eminently practical man.

CHAPTER 7

Baker's Legacy

WE MAY well hesitate to pronounce judgment on a mystic or his works, for the meaning of a contemplative's life is hidden and interior, while the validity of his writings can be fully understood only by another mystic. Perhaps the only really valid test of a book like *Sancta Sophia* is to put it to use in the way it was intended—as a practical guide to the contemplative way—and to see if it works. If the book evades easy judgment by rational methods, then evaluation of its author must be even more difficult. Therefore, the critic must proceed warily. "A Carthusian or a Trappist," writes Bernanos, "will work for years to make of himself a man of prayer, and then any fool who comes along sets himself up as a judge of this lifelong effort." [1] Nevertheless, in spite of these cautions, it is necessary to attempt an evaluation of Baker's writings, of his effect on others, and of his importance and genuineness as a mystic.

I *Baker's Influence*

Baker did not directly influence English poetry or literary prose to any significant extent. In the seventeenth century, as Elbert Thompson points out, "the undercurrent of mysticism came strongly to the surface" in English literature, but it is frequently mysticism of a rather vague kind; "formal mysticism has not thriven naturally on English soil." [2] Thompson presumably means by "formal mysticism" something like that described in Chapter 3 of this study. Some of the reasons for an absence of this kind of mysticism from English poetry have been suggested—the dissolution of the monasteries which were the institutional base for contemplation; the mistrust of personal, charismatic religion caused by the excesses of zealots; the growth of rationalism. Puritans, who by temperament were most individualistic, also were most strongly prejudiced against formal contemplation. Only in recent years has the mystic element in seventeenth-century literature received anything approaching rigorous examination, and it may be that mysticism will be found to have played a broader role than previously thought. It is a difficult subject to treat, for it tends to escape categorization or analysis; yet more is needed than impressionistic surveys, or the eclectic culling of passages, two pitfalls into which many of the earlier studies fell.

It is beyond the scope of this book to comment more than briefly on mysticism in seventeenth-century English literature, but a few figures can be mentioned. Most obvious are Henry Vaughan and Thomas Traherne, who have received attention from a number of critics. There is no question that these poets were, each in his own way, mystics by natural inclination or supernatural gift. Unmistakable signs of formal—if derivative—mysticism can also be found in several poems of Francis Quarles.[3] Richard Crashaw was influenced by the tradition and borrows its imagery.

None of these writers were mystics, however, in the same sense as Baker, perhaps because the gift of mysticism must be followed with single-mindedness and enormous self-sacrifice before advancement is possible. If Vaughan, for example, like Baker, received the gift of a "propension" to the contemplative life and underwent some kind of mystical experience, he appears to have gradually lost it instead of pursuing it at all costs. The diminution over the years of his power to write mystical poetry (although not absolutely certain) has often been noted—as if he were working from reminiscences of a single experience or of a period of fervor that was fading into the past. Certitude in such matters is, of course, impossible; and little is known of Vaughan's outward life, still less of his spiritual state. But, by setting the writings of figures like Vaughan and Traherne against the touchstone of Baker's work, it is possible to see the difference between intimations or reminiscences of the mystical state and a full dedication to the contemplative way.

For a study of mysticism in seventeenth-century English poetry it would be desirable, if difficult, to differentiate between the influence of the English contemplative tradition and that subsequently imported from the Continent. The difference is mainly one of tone and symbolism, rather than doctrine: thus, generally speaking, the use of fiery and emotional imagery like Crashaw's indicates a Continental influence (in fact, as we know, St. Teresa was decisively important to him); and the use of calmer and more restrained language—more light than fire, as in Vaughan's poems—is more typically English. Baker is significant to English literature, not because of any direct influence on it, but because he is the most important English mystic of the period; as such he throws light on the less clearly expressed mysticism of other writers.

Baker's influence on his own order of Benedictines is clearer; it is evident from the time of his death to the present. He had many friends and disciples at Cambray and Douay during his life. His death, instead of diminishing his influence, increased it, although this influence was accompanied by the same controversy that he had aroused while alive. According to a recent commentary, "after Baker's death in 1641 all might have been forgiven and forgotten had not an astonishing cultus of Father Baker sprung up among English people. He was at once styled Venerable, and within a few years numerous Lives had been written and circulated, so that his influence, far from waning, seemed ever on the increase."[4] The title page of *Sancta Sophia* (1657) refers to Baker as "the late Ven. Father," so the use of this honorific was sanctioned by the English Benedictine Chapter. This spreading interest in Baker had actually begun before his death; for, as Justin McCann points out, the publication of *Sancta Sophia* was the culmination of a whole series of unofficial compendiums and extract books made by Baker's disciples and passed around in manuscript.[5]

Cressy was delegated to edit Baker's works by the General Chapter of 1653. In 1655, however, the president of the English Congregation, Fr. Claude White, tried to get Dame Catherine Gascoigne, the Abbess of Cambray, to surrender Baker's manuscripts to him for examination and possible revision—as we know through some peripheral correspondence that fell into the hands of the English government. The nuns politely but firmly refused to hand over the manuscripts on the ground that they had been approved by the official action of a General Chapter, so that only another General Chapter could revoke that approval. In the course of the dispute, Fr. White came to Cambray, where Dame Catherine reports that he told her "the books are declared to containe poysonous, pernicious and diabolicall doctrine, myselfe [Dame Catherine] in a damnable way running to perdition."[6]

These words, recently interpreted as meaning that Baker's doctrines were suspected of Quietism, were obviously spoken in anger and were calculated to frighten the nuns into obedience rather than to inform the historian. The exact cause of Fr. White's action is really unkown, but there are grounds to suspect that Fr. Rudisind Barlow may have been responsible for this vendetta. The outcome of the quarrel was settled by death; for, as Dom Justin McCann points out, "Fr Claude White died in the autumn of 1655, Fr Rudisind in 1656; *Sancta Sophia* was happily published in 1657." [7] Whatever the nature of the charges against Baker's writings, Fr. White and Fr. Barlow cannot have had much confidence in their validity, or they would not have permitted the General Chapter of 1653 to order Cressy, unanimously and without argument, to prepare *Sancta Sophia* for publication. At this time, both men remained silent.

Baker's influence had spread beyond his own congregation even before his death. We have seen that the Carmelites of Antwerp, having read his works, asked him in 1638 to be their spiritual director. We also know that Baker wrote a manuscript entitled *A Summary of Perfection*, dated April 10, 1638, which is dedicated to "the V. R. Mother Abbess of the English religious of the holy Order of St. Clare in the town of Aire, Mother Catherine Keynes, as composed by the author principally for her sake." [8] Obviously, word of Baker's method was spreading beyond his own order. In 1641, he was honored indirectly by the appointment of his disciple, Dame Catherine Gascoigne, to be temporary superior of the French nuns of St. Lazare in Cambray. Archbishop Vanderburch, who admired the way things were run at the English convent, asked her to help the French nuns reform. She was accompanied on this mission by Dame Bridget More, sister of Dame Gertrude, and by Dame Clementia Cary, eldest daughter of Viscount Falkland (whose chaplain had once been Serenus Cressy, before Cressy's conversion); all were Bakerists.[9] Indeed, it is fascinating to trace the spreading circles of converts that owed their conversions indirectly to Baker, although we cannot indulge in the details here. His converts seemed to acquire from him the ability to make other converts, an ability evidently closely associated with the nature of Bakerism and its approach to prayer and spiritual freedom.

Baker's method had worked conspicuously well with the nuns of Cambray; and, in the record of the relationship between Baker and Dame Gertrude More, published in the *Inner Life,* we have a unique example of Baker's doctrine being put to practical use. Dom Philibert Schmitz writes: "We really have here 'a doctrine in action, controlled and modified by all the reactions of life', a situation that is very rare in the history of spirituality." [10] Because the era was one of religious ferment, many of the nuns in Europe took Jesuits as their confessors in order to be doctrinally safe. Peter Guilday points out that "it is owing to Father Baker's wonderful direction that, whereas all the English foundations of contemplative nuns in the Low Countries sought to safeguard themselves from . . . Jansenism and Quietism, by taking Jesuits for their confessors and directors, and made the doing so a part of their constitutions,—the Benedictine nuns of Cambrai alone never had recourse to the Society for guidance." [11]

In England, *Sancta Sophia* was read by at least a few people. John Worthington, who discussed Baker in a letter to Henry More, the Cambridge Platonist, wrote rather sharply (and apparently in answer to the suggestion that he valued Baker too highly) that "besides the mark of the beast, the Popery in Aug. Baker's books, there is a deal of stuff, when he treats of Contemplation and its parts, Unions active and passive, &c. that to me is insignificant. He seems to me to talk in divinity (as to such points) as Plotinus talks in his Philosophy, things not to be seen, felt, or understood." But, surprisingly, Dr. Worthington found it possible to like much of *Sancta Sophia* without liking contemplation or mysticism. What he approved is Baker's psychology and his approach to asceticism:

But the picture of Aug. Baker which I like, is the picture of his serious thoughts, his affectionate sentiments; and where he meddles not with any of the particular doctrines, modes and rites of the Romish Church, but delivers himself concerning such practical matters and experimental truths, as those who are most inwardly and seriously religious do agree in and heartily relish. To me he seems to represent them so properly, so powerfully and clearly, and so unaffectedly . . . that I know but few Protestants do better, or write with such life and energy, and in so spirituall a strain, and so searchingly about mortification and self-abnegation, to the discovery of selfness and nature in her many close interests and designs, and most secret insinuations.[12]

There are affinities between orthodox Christian mysticism and English Neoplatonism, as well as with the hermetic doctrines associated with the latter. It is difficult, for example, to separate the various religious and philosophical influences on Henry Vaughan. Therefore, the possibility that Henry More was acquainted with *Sancta Sophia* is interesting and, perhaps, significant.

In addition to John Worthington, and possibly Henry More, we know that the Quaker Robert Barclay read at least part of *Sancta Sophia*. There are two other early instances of Baker's influence in England outside his Congregation. Lady Abigail Fairfax, who died in 1710, was "'much given to internal prayer and retirement' using 'Dame Gertrude Moores book and (Fr. Augustine Baker's) Sancta Sophia'" as spiritual guides. A less sympathetic reader of *Sancta Sophia* was William Nicholls, who in a preface to his bowlderization of *An Introduction to a Devout Life* by St. Francis de Sales, published in 1701, remarked that St. Francis "*does not run into the Mystical stuff of* Teresa, Blosius, Sancta Sophia, &c.," which he subsequently characterizes as "*Bedlam Divinity*." [13] This casual reference to *Sancta Sophia*, without mentioning the author, argues that Nicholls expected his readers to have heard of the book. Baker's audience cannot have been wide, however, since the second impression promised by Cressy, "if we shall be encouraged thereto," never appeared.[14] Yet in the following centuries, Baker's influence, far from dying, continued to grow.

In the eighteenth century, records about Baker are few; but one remains to attest to his lasting influence among the English Benedictine nuns. It is from the obituary of Reverend Mother Teresa Johnson, who was elected superior of the daughter house of Cambray in Paris, one year after the beginning of the French Revolution, and who after much suffering died in England on August 31, 1807: "She was of a most peaceful, cheerful temper, the life and soul of the Community, and filled with burning ardor and love for our holy Institute, Intern Prayer, and Contemplation ever seeking the union of the Soul with God, and saying with Father Baker—*'Mind your call that's all in all*." [15]

About the middle of the nineteenth century we hear of Baker once more, and from this report it is evident that controversy still had not died out. According to Dom James Laurence Shepherd, who became novice master at Ampleforth in 1852, "One of the elders warned me against Father Baker. . . . But I took him from the library, and became enamoured of his style. . . . I epitomized *Sancta Sophia* and passed it thus to my novices." [16] While the opposition to Bakerism lived on, so did Baker's teachings.

In the second half of the nineteenth century, a number of publications appeared, beginning with an edition of *Sancta Sophia* in 1857 and including Sweeney's *Life* (1861) and the 1876 edition of *Sancta Sophia*. The twentieth century has seen numerous printings of *Sancta Sophia*, the *Lives* edited by Justin McCann, and many summaries of Baker's teachings, together with renewed critical interest. The reader is referred to the Selected Bibliography for details. Aside from the growing number of publications, Baker's influence is still a living tradition. The Benedictine nuns of Stanbrook Abbey, formerly Cambray, write of *Sancta Sophia:*

Its method, deeply imbued with the spirit of St. Benedict, combines shrewd insight with devastating commonsense, insisting above all on the need for recollection and on the freedom and fidelity of the soul in its response to the demands of Divine grace, and making no concession to ill-balanced mysticism or to that appetite for the marvellous which so often seems to accompany it. The result is a certain peaceful integration of the whole personality in the service of God, a simple, thorough-going, unspectacular holiness which we have seen, for instance, clearly marked in Dame Catherine Gascoigne, but which has also been discernable in many, many another English Benedictine monk and nun during the intervening three centuries.[17]

This description of the nature of Bakerism is of interest as it is presumably based on practical experience with Baker's method. Together with three or four mystical treatises of the fourteenth century, *Sancta Sophia* remains a textbook of English mysticism. A glance at the selected Bibliography also shows that it is read on the Continent, particularly in France.

The unpolemical nature of Baker's work is evidenced by the fact that *Sancta Sophia* has in recent years been used by Anglicans as well as by Catholics. The Anglican Abbot of Pershore, in an article on contemplation, wrote: "Though too much has been made of the influence of nationality on devotion, English devotion will be well advised in not departing from Augustine Baker's *Sancta Sophia* as a standard book on prayer." [18] Much of the "mark of the beast" that Dr. Worthington objected to now seems innocuous, so that, while many of the controversial books of the period are today only historical curiosities, Baker's work has a wider audience than it had in the seventeenth century. *Sancta Sophia* is also recognized in the more eclectic books on mysticism: Evelyn Underhill calls it "one of the most lucid and orderly of guides to the contemplative life," while Geraldine Hodgson goes so far as to say that "Augustine Baker and Gertrude More . . . fill a place in the story of English religious life extraordinarily like that which is occupied in the roll of Spanish Mystics by S. Teresa and . . . S. John of the Cross." [19] This judgment is carrying national partisanship a long way, but Baker does hold an important place in English mysticism.

The literary histories, although they have somewhat slighted Baker, recognize his role as the only important English Catholic mystic of his era. Douglas Bush, writing in the *Oxford History of English Literature,* calls him "the chief Roman Catholic mystic of our period," while W. H. Hutton in *The Cambridge History of English Literature* assigns him two pages of comment. [20] The greater part of the published work concerning Baker, however, still comes from his fellow Benedictines. Among them Baker's work has been increasingly important and influential; for, as Abbot Cuthbert Butler points out, *Sancta Sophia* has at least a semi-official authority: it "was no private venture." [21]

II *Recent Controversy*

Nevertheless, in spite of these credentials and in spite of his widening influence, the controversy surrounding Baker has not ended. Criticism has come mainly from two directions: from certain French commentators, and from Professor David Knowles. The French criticism stems from the work of Dom Paul Renaudin, who published an article on Baker in 1938, later incorporating it in his book, *Quatre Mystiques Anglais; Richard Rolle, Juliane de Norwich, Dom Augustin Baker, Gertrude More* (Paris, 1945). Renaudin charges that Baker lived in community for only a few years, and even then stayed in his cell; that he did not sing the office with the other monks; that he was by nature difficult to get along with and not a good "community man"—very important for a Benedictine. In rebuttal, we may point out that Baker made firm friends wherever he went—at Cambray, at Douay, and even during his short stay at Padua. His friends and disciples far outnumbered his critics. As for living in community, the times and his poor health were against it. He celebrated mass daily between 1624 and 1638, not a universal practice at that time, which shows his respect for the liturgy and public prayer of the Church.

Behind the charge of being a bad community man stands another question: what St. Benedict meant by the *Opus Dei,* the prayer which is the work of God and to which all Benedictine monks must give first priority. Some Benedictines argue that the singing of the Office is all-important, that mental prayer can be largely dispensed with, and that properly used the Office itself provides the material for contemplation. On the other side are those, among them Baker, who insist on at least one, and preferably two, periods of individual mental prayer every day. In Baker's time the Office and the Liturgy were fully developed and consumed a great deal of time, while, during the course of the eighteenth and nineteenth centuries, mental prayer and individual spirituality played greater and greater roles, until in the early twentieth century the balance was once more redressed. Therefore, just as Baker overemphasized the importance of will in prayer because in his time discursive prayer was disproportionately popular, so he may occasionally have overemphasized private prayer at the expense of the Office for the same reason.[22]

Renaudin also refers to Baker as a converted Protestant, evidently not understanding the shades of opinion and conviction in seventeenth-century England. Baker, even at Christ's Hospital, never was much taken with Anglicanism, so that it would be more accurate to say that he was raised a Church Papist, or as he himself says, that he became a "practical Atheist." Renaudin's insistence that Baker's doctrines of inspiration and spiritual liberty are Protestant in origin are therefore erroneous.[23] Baker's ideal of liberty stems, not from English Protestant theories, which were in any case not fully developed during his youth, but from the freedom of the soul insisted on by the great mystics—the freedom that St. John of the Cross demands so that God, the master painter, can work as he pleases.

If Renaudin is critical of Baker's life and doctrine, however, his opinion is relatively unimportant in comparison with the heavier attack leveled against Baker by David Knowles. The variety of Professor Knowles's charges make them difficult to answer. Some answer is, nevertheless, necessary because Professor Knowles's opinion is weighty and at present stands unchallenged.[24]

One device that Knowles uses is indirect criticism, or damnation by faint praise. He writes, for example, that "exteriorly he may seem narrow and his ways unlovely; but his doctrine is all love, and he gives as a guide God's Holy Spirit." [25] It may be unfair to point out contradictions among Knowles's various essays on Baker, since opinions naturally change over a period of years. Two examples ought to be given, however, because they involve central points in his argument. One is his attack, referred to in Chapter 4, on Baker's prayer of acts of the will, in which Knowles charges that these acts are just as elementary a form of prayer as meditation, that Baker "is at fault when he describes the prayer of the will, *tout court,* as 'contemplative'." [26] We have already seen that Baker does not do so, and therefore we may feel that Knowles's judgment in 1927 was more accurate: "Yet perhaps his greatest addition to Catholic mystical literature is his sane and lucid instruction in the first stage of contemplative prayer, acts of the will and aspirations. Indeed, in the fulness of his analysis of the first degree, acts of the will, he stands alone. No other spiritual writer, uninspired by him, is so clear and helpful."

In 1927, Professor Knowles wrote that "there are no digressions, no chapters that can be isolated from the rest . . . *Sancta Sophia* is an organic whole";[27] in 1962, that "despite the efforts of Fr Cressy's 'methodical digestion' it remains a heap rather than a block or a building, and there are many chapters, valuable and indeed indispensable, which cannot be pressed into any logical order." [28] That judgments change over a period of thirty-five years is not surprising; but it is harder to understand how chapters can be "valuable and indeed indispensable," yet completely digressive. It is also difficult to see how the book can be accused of a basic lack of order at the same time that one "feels rather than sees in *Sancta Sophia* something of the cold logic that repels, even while it fascinates, in the great Arnauld." [29] Arnauld, the author of *Frequent Communion,* a seminal work in the Jansenist movement, was a neo-Augustinian or predestinarian—a kind of Catholic Calvin. But, if Baker is accused of "cold logic" of this sort, is the charge consistent with his supposed inability to put his work into "logical order," let alone with the fact of his many warm friendships?

Knowles points to a passage in *Sancta Sophia* that he believes illustrates Baker's unfortunate attitude toward obedience to his superiors: "Also you may hope to have a good cross superior, if you pray hard for having such a one, or that God will see it necessary to send you such a one who shall break and contradict your wills." This passage is used to illustrate what Knowles thinks is an essentially negative attitude toward the discipline of community life. Sister St. Teresa Higgins pointed out to me in a conversation, however, that these words were addressed to the nuns of Cambray, whose superior, Dame Catherine Gascoigne (a disciple of Baker's), was no doubt a member of the audience. It is safe to assume that Baker is being humorous; in fact, there are many passages in *Sancta Sophia* that may be suspected of humor. It is never obtrusive, but my own impression of Baker as he reveals himself in his works is one of warmth rather than of coldness.

That Baker was a poor community man, a solitary, "aloof and ungenial," [30] "humourless," "a man of whimsies and corners," has, I think, already been refuted. Another charge, that "he never writes as a trained theologian," can be balanced against the criticism that "he was a scholar rather than an autodidact." [31] Both Professor Knowles and Dom Gerard Sitwell argue that much of Baker's teaching is derived from other writers; that he did not understand what he was writing; that he was not really a mystic in the strict experiential sense of the word. Possibly Baker did not perfectly understand, before 1638, the very highest reaches of mysticism; but the history of his life clearly shows that an inner urge, not reading, first led him to mysticism; and his style reveals that he really felt what he was saying, that he was not just setting down words.

It might be said that there are two kinds of mystics: those who from childhood are drawn to an inner world of their own, who hear some call that most men do not; and those who are first introduced to mysticism later in life through the agency of a book, or of another person. Dame Gertrude More, for example, did not have the faintest conception of what the mystical life was about until Baker showed her, and at first she resisted him. Yet the genuineness of her subsequent mystical life cannot be doubted. For although there are many paths to mysticism, there is no essential difference in the nature of that mysticism once arrived at. It is unimportant what originally came from books, what from within. Usually even an ordinary reader can tell the difference between the work of a genuine mystic, however conventional his terminology, and that of someone who understands mysticism only intellectually—just as the work of a genuine poet, though he write in a conventional tradition, is distinguishable from that of a mere versifier.

It would have been impossible for Baker, if he were not a mystic, to have sustained the impression through so many treatises that he understood and was deeply committed to what he was writing about. If his writings were merely pieced together from the scraps of other mystics, then they would have a dullness and a lifelessness that no fair reader can find in them. Professor Knowles acknowledges that *Sancta Sophia* has withstood the test of close examination and long use, which is probably more reliable than the theoretical opinion of a non-mystic (such as I). Knowles reports: "It is indeed one of the very few spiritual masterpieces that can be read again and again, and serve as a life's guide. The late Abbot Cuthbert Butler read it at least once a year for more than fifty years on end." [32] It is best to close our examination of the critical attack against Baker on this positive note.

III   *Conclusions*

Because Baker refused to involve himself in the intricate religious arguments of his period, his writings have lost little or nothing of their pertinence; and they do not suffer from the opposite fault of remoteness or overabstraction because they are solidly based on his experience and on that of his spiritual charges. He did not withdraw himself from the problems of Catholicism in his time. He exposed himself to arrest along with his more active confreres, doing whatever he was enjoined to by his duty. When he left England, at the invitation of his superior, he did so in order to avoid unnecessary distraction in his spiritual life. He has been called "a contemplative spirit who progressively withdrew from the outer, national struggle for religious freedom, yet who was deeply committed to the most profound aspects of that struggle." [33]

E. I. Watkin has suggested a useful way of looking at Catholic activities in England: "Throughout this period the Papacy fought a it were with the right and the left hands. The right hand was spiritual . . . confirming the faithful, reconciling the lapsed, ministering the sacraments. The left hand was political, the employment of political and military weapons." [34] Both the Recusants and the English government frequently confused the political and the spiritual. The two were sometimes so closely intertwined that it would have been difficult not to have done so, for state religions and established churches, in one form or another, were characteristic of the times.

Nothing in Baker's life or his writings, however, sacrifices the spiritual to political considerations, so that he may be thought of as an admirable exemplar of "right-handed" action. Not that all the political activity of the Recusants was reprehensible; but, in a sense, Baker's activity was actually more practical and had better results. Helen C. White pictures the contrast between his life and that of some of the more politically inclined Recusants: "It is surely not without significance that perhaps the most notable figure of the age of hidden and even buried life that was in the new century to succeed the culminating disaster of the English Mission, the Gunpowder Plot . . . was to be a great contemplative, the Benedictine Augustine Baker." [35]

Baker, in his treatises and in his life, reached back into the past, taking the writings of the Fathers and of previous mystics for his guides. According to Abbott Butler, "Fr Baker, if I mistake not, may rightly be regarded as the last of the line of great medieval mystics." [36] Baker's commentary on the late medieval *Cloud of Unknowing* is still helpful in understanding that work, and yet to be replaced. But it would be misleading to push this resemblance too far. For Baker was also a man of his own time, who was engaged with its problems and who revealed no trace of longing for the past. He was not a romantic; he characteristically kept his balance in all that he wrote, not retreating from reality, but refusing to be swayed by controversy. Moreover, he was fully conscious of the spiritual currents of his age: of the needs of the English Congregation, of the methods of prayer being used in Europe, of the latest work of other contemplatives. Although we might now place more emphasis on St. John of the Cross, Baker shows a remarkable instinct in the writings of which he makes use; for, during this era, there was a bewildering profusion of spiritual books.

Although he lacked ambition, he was by the test of time the only member of his congregation who had an enduring influence. "Indeed," he wrote, "true internal livers are not very solicitous for gaining credit and esteem with the world, and much less would they make that an end of their religious observances. On the contrary, their cordial desire is to live unknown and excluded from the world, approving their souls to God only" (*Sancta Sophia,* 1.3.5.11). The words that Mother Christina Brent applied negatively to someone else describe Baker well: he was "versed in the words of S. John Baptist: 'I am not'" (Salvin and Cressy, xxxi).

Baker's disciple, Dame Gertrude More, in her last years underwent much testing, criticism, and opposition; but she persevered to her death in the way that Baker had taught her. Speaking of these trials in the *Inner Life,* Baker wrote: "To be persecuted by evil persons is a kind of honour, for it will be supposed that justice is on the side of the one attacked, and this makes amends for the bitterness of the persecution. But if the aggressor be good, or esteemed to be good, then, in addition to the bitterness of the persecution, there will be a certain degree of discredit, for people generally will believe that justice lies on the other side" (136–37).

These words are ironically appropriate to the man who wrote them, for they describe perfectly the collision between Baker and Fr. Rudisind Barlow. At first the result seemed to be a victory for Barlow, but in the end Baker and his doctrines were vindicated. History is full of instances of contemplatives who have been ignored or, more frequently, attacked during their lifetimes, but who have gained posthumous victories over their critics. Perhaps the verdict of the nuns of Cambray is best, however; for in "A Register of such Benefactors as have notably advanced the Spiritual or Temporal Good of his Convent," appear the names of both disputants: "Austin Baker" and "F. Rudesind." [37]

Rufus Jones writes that "the great mystics are religious geniuses. They make their contributions to religion in ways similar to those in which the geniuses in other fields raise the level of human attainments and achievements." [38] The equivalence of religious genius with genius in other fields is disputable, because of the part that may be played by divine inspiration or grace; but the comparison is still useful. The mark of a genius is his ability to rise above the preoccupations of his time and culture, to produce something new or to revive something forgotten. At the same time, if his work is not to be ignored, he must have a thorough grasp of the needs of his time or of the future. Both these characteristics fit Baker, for they involve just that kind of balance that we have remarked in him.

Baker's influence has been less overt or observable than that of the scientific geniuses of his time; but it is no less real, and possibly no less important. The impact of religion, like that of literature or the humanities, is hard to pin down; in a sense, it is too pervasive. Spiritual ideals, and particularly contemplative ideals, are propagated in men's inner lives, where they are not visible to the historian; but their fruits are nonetheless significant. How far a religious talent like Baker's is due to natural gifts, how far to supernatural, is beyond the scope of this study, although Baker himself believed that grace manifested and perfected natural tendencies and abilities, so that both natural and supernatural combine in a mystic. At any rate, we may say that he was both a genuine mystic and an unusually lucid interpreter of mysticism to others.

His persuasive call to contemplation and the spiritual life, his emphasis on simple prayer of the will rather than on formal meditation, his combination of unlimited goals with moderation in approaching them, and above all his insistence on following the guidance of divine inspiration along the unique, individual path that each soul must take are all traditional and orthodox. But sometimes it takes great insight to return to traditional simplicity in a time of complexity, to ignore the exigencies of controversy but nevertheless perceive the needs underlying that controversy. Augustine Baker had this kind of insight, as well as the ability to pass on his ideas to others around him. He had the gifts of spiritual vision and of communication. Most important, he was favored with the desire to seek God directly and experientially, above all other goals. During the last twenty years of his life he never turned from the contemplative way, exemplifying in action his own advice: "Mind your call: that's all in all."

Notes and References

Chapter One

1. Ronald A. Knox, *Enthusiasm* (Oxford, 1950), pp. 231–32.
2. "Father Augustine Baker," in *English Spiritual Writers*, ed. Charles Davis (New York, 1962), p. 102.
3. *Memorials of Father Augustine Baker and Other Documents Relating to the English Benedictines*, ed. Justin McCann and Hugh Connolly, Catholic Record Society, XXXIII (London, 1933), 274–93 (hereafter cited as *Memorials* in the text); Peter Salvin and Serenus Cressy, *The Life of Father Augustine Baker, O.S.B.*, ed. Justin McCann (London, 1933), pp. 160–201 (cited as Salvin or Cressy); and Justin McCann, "Ten More Baker MSS.," *Ampleforth Journal*, LXIII (1958), 77–83.
4. J. Norbert Sweeney, *The Life & Spirit of Father Augustine Baker* (London, 1861).
5. Pritchard's life is in *Memorials*, 53–154.
6. *The Confessions of Venerable Father Augustine Baker, O.S.B.*, ed. Justin McCann (London, 1922). Hereafter cited as *Confessions*.
7. *The Inner Life and the Writings of Dame Gertrude More*, rev. and ed. Dom Benedict Weld-Blundell, 2 vols. (London, 1910–11). Hereafter cited as *Inner Life*.
8. See Dom Justin McCann, "Father Baker's Dame Gertrude," *Downside Review*, XLVII (1929), 157–67.
9. Justin McCann, "Father Baker's Tercentenary," *Downside Review*, LIX (1941), 360.
10. Both in *Memorials*.
11. *The Cloud of Unknowing . . . With a Commentary on the Cloud by Father Augustine Baker*, ed. Abbot Justin McCann (Westminster, Md., 1952). Hereafter cited as *Commentary on the Cloud* or *Commentary*.
12. "Of Finding God Within Our Soul," *Downside Review*, LX (1942), 23–32.
13. McCann, "Father Baker's Tercentenary."
14. *English Devotional Literature 1600–1640*, Univ. of Wis. Stud. in Lang. and Lit., No. 29 (Madison, 1931), p. 10.

15. See Louis Martz, *The Poetry of Meditation* (New Haven, 1962), pp. 4–13.

16. Elbert N. S. Thompson, "Mysticism in Seventeenth-Century English Literature," *Studies in Philology*, XVIII (1921), 170–231; Itrat Husain, *The Mystical Element in the Metaphysical Poets of the Seventeenth Century* (Edinburgh, 1948); Robert A. Durr, *On the Mystical Poetry of Henry Vaughan* (Cambridge, Mass., 1962); K. W. Salter, *Thomas Traherne: Mystic and Poet* (New York, 1964).

17. McCann, "Father Baker's Tercentenary," p. 357.

18. Edward Ingram Watkin, *The Philosophy of Mysticism* (London, 1920), p. 31.

19. McCann, "Augustine Baker," p. 94.

20. See Salvin and Cressy, Appendix II, pp. 160–201.

21. *Sancta Sophia*, ed. J. Norbert Sweeney (London, 1876), p. 206. This edition is used throughout.

Chapter Two

1. Fr. Leander Norminton, "On the Picture and Writings of the late venerable F. Augustin Baker," *Sancta Sophia*, opposite frontispiece.

2. *Ibid.*

3. David Knowles, "Father Augustine Baker," pp. 97–111.

4. Pritchard writes that William Baker was "Sheriffe of Monmouthshire" (*Memorials*, 54). But Baker's name does not appear in the list of sheriffs in Thomas Nicholas, "High Sheriffs of Monmouthshire, A.D. 1541–1872," *Annals and Antiquities of the Counties and County Families of Wales*, II (London, 1872), 759–64.

5. T. P. Ellis, *The Welsh Benedictines of the Terror* (Newtown, Wales, 1936), Appendix III, n. p.

6. Such as the Elizabethan equivalent of the Catholic office book, *The Primer set forth at large, with many godly and devout prayers, Anno, 1559*. Cited by Helen White, "Some Continuing Traditions in English Devotional Literature," *Publications of the Modern Language Association*, LVII (1942), 972n.

7. E. I. Watkin, *Roman Catholicism in England from the Reformation to 1950* (London, 1957), pp. 20, 33–34.

8. *Ibid.*, p. 64.

9. See [Cooke], *Students Admitted to the Inner Temple, 1547–1660* (London, 1877), p. 146.

10. Most writers on Baker, including Fr. McCann, assume the river is the Monnow, but I. D. Griffith Davies, in "The Catholic Nonconformists of Monmouthshire," *The Monmouthshire Review*, II (1934), 154n, says the Monnow is too small to fit Baker's description, but the Usk could be the river in question.

11. Sister St. Teresa Higgins, "Augustine Baker," unpublished doctoral dissertation (Univ. of Wisconsin, 1963), p. 37.

12. Leys, *Catholics in England 1559–1829; A Social History* (London, 1961), p. 19. Baker himself warns superiors to beware of false pleas of ill health by monks who want to go on the English mission (*Sancta Sophia*, 191).

13. It is uncertain whether Buckley was imprisoned again after 1603. For a discussion of the incident that prints the original sources, see Hugh Connolly, "The Buckley Affair," *Downside Review*, XLIX (1931), 49–74. Fr. Connolly decides against the tradition that Buckley was in prison at the time of the aggregation, but the sources are confused.

14. See Baker's "Treatise of the Mission" in *Memorials*, p. 163; and Connolly, "The Buckley Affair," p. 64.

15. Cuthbert Fursdon in turn converted Cressy, Baker's future biographer and editor of *Sancta Sophia*.

16. Anthony Wood, *Athenae Oxonienses*, second edition (London, 1721), II, 8.

17. Before the Union took place, English Benedictines belonged to either the Italian or the Spanish congregations. Since the Englishmen in the Spanish Congregation far outnumbered the others, one condition of union put the English Congregation under of the Spanish. This seemed the best arrangement for a small group in exile. The Italian Benedictine monks, however, would not accept it, so the very men who brought the union about refused to join. Baker was an exception.

18. See "Records of the Abbey of Our Lady of Consolation at Cambrai, 1620–1793," ed. Joseph Gillow, *Miscellanea VIII*, Catholic Record Society, XIII (London, 1913), 41–44.

19. Henry Ellis, *Original Letters*, Second Series, III (London, 1827), 256–58.

20. *Sancta Sophia*, title page.

21. See Robert W. Gleason, S.J., ed., *The Spiritual Exercises of St. Ignatius* (New York, 1964), pp. 16, 23–24.

22. Higgins, "Augustine Baker," p. 114.

23. For the historical portion of this treatise see *Memorials*, 155–185. The spiritual advice is summarized in *Sancta Sophia* (1.3.10).

24. See Philip Hughes, *Rome and the Counter-Reformation in England* (London, 1942), p. 357 and note.

25. See *Sancta Sophia* (1.3.8) for the ills caused by "active" monks.

26. See Connolly, "Two Official Relations," *Memorials*, p. 270. The report sent to Spain by the English Congregation in 1637 states that Douay "will be obliged to reduce by half the number of religious which ordinarily they are accustomed to have."

27. *Ibid.*

Chapter Three

1. From the title page of *Sancta Sophia* (1657).

2. St. John of the Cross, *Works*, I, 105 (*Ascent of Mount Carmel*, II.xii.4).

3. Abbé P. Lejeune, *An Introduction to the Mystical Life*, trans. Basil Levett (London, 1915), p. 7. Lejeune quotes from Poulain, *The Graces of Interior Prayer*, n.p.

4. Cited by Watkin, *Philosophy of Mysticism*, p. 131.

5. *Ibid.*, p. 242.

6. For the Continental background of meditation and its English literary uses, see Louis Martz, *The Poetry of Meditation* (New Haven, 1954).

7. Abbot Cuthbert Butler, *Western Mysticism* (London, 1927), pp. xviii–xx.

8. *Ibid.*, p. xx. But see David Knowles, *The English Mystical Tradition* (New York, 1961), p. 163.

9. St. Thomas Aquinas, *Summa Theologica*, trans. Fathers of the English Dominican Province, 3 vols. (New York, 1946–48), p. 1935 (Pt. II–II, Q.180,A.5).

10. St. Augustine, *The Confessions*, trans. Edward B. Pusey (New York, 1949), pp. 133–34.

11. Watkin, *Philosophy of Mysticism*, p. 209.

12. *Ibid.*, pp. 245–46.

13. St. Teresa, *Works*, I, xxviii; *Sancta Sophia* (3.1.7.6).

14. *Sancta Sophia* (1.3.4.19); see also (1.3.4.20). Leander Jones ("Memorial," *Sancta Sophia*, p. 556) supports Baker.

15. *Summa*, p. 1943 (Pt. II–II,Q.182,A.1); p. 1941 (Pt. II–II, Q.181,A.4).

16. See David Knowles, "Father Augustine Baker," in *English Spiritual Writers*, ed. C. Davis, p. 109; and Gerard Sitwell, Introduction to his edition of *Holy Wisdom* (London, 1964), pp. viii–ix; hereafter referred to as *Holy Wisdom* (1964). One passage contradicting these charges is *Sancta Sophia* (3.4.6.11).

17. See, for example, George Williamson, "Mutability, Decay, and Jacobean Melancholy," *Seventeen Century Contexts* (London, 1960), pp. 9–41; or Herschel Baker, *The Wars of Truth* (Cambridge, Mass., 1952), pp. 65–78.

18. *Holy Wisdom* (1964), pp. x–xi.

19. Unless God Himself quiets the soul, imposing an inability to act or to pray discursively, called "the ligature." But this would presumably occur at the border between acts and aspirations. Butler (*Western Mysticism*, pp. xxxvi–xxxix) writes that Baker's prayer of aspirations is compatible with St. John's loving attention.

20. *Sancta Sophia* (3.3.1.19). This probably refers to the "ligature" —see previous note—a term current shortly after Baker's time (first used in a letter from St. Francis de Sales to St. Jane Francis de Chantal).

21. "Of Finding God Within Our Soul," *Downside Review*, LX–LXI (1942–43), 29.

22. By the image of the writing master Baker distinguishes between "active" contemplation in which the soul is the agent *together* with God, and "passive" contemplation, in which "God becometh the sole worker" (*Confessions*, p. 61).

23. From Justin McCann, "Father Baker's Tercentenary," *Downside Review*, LIX (1941), 369–70.

24. Quoted "from an unpublished passage of the *Secretum*" by E. I. Watkin in *Poets and Mystics* (London, 1953), p. 206. See also *Sancta Sophia*. (3.4.6.9).

25. Watkin (*Poets and Mystics*, p. 204) calls it a "substantial locution," from St. John of the Cross, *Ascent*, Bk. II, Ch. 31. He discusses thoroughly Baker's use of "active" and "passive" as applied to contemplation or union (pp. 203–25).

26. Sitwell, ed., *Holy Wisdom* (1964), p. xi; Knowles, "Father Augustine Baker," p. 109.

27. That is, if we use the terms "active" and "passive" as they are commonly employed—although they are sometimes inadequate. Watkin (*Poets and Mystics*, pp. 203–25) assumes Baker was consciously modifying the traditional terminology, but it was probably more an accident than a new philosophy of mysticism—though his doctrine agrees with tradition once his peculiar use of the terms is understood.

Chapter Four

1. Browne, *Religio Medici and Other Works*, ed. L. C. Martin (Oxford, 1964), p. 19 (i.19).

2. Burton, *The Anatomy of Melancholy*, ed. Holbrook Jackson (London, 1932), I, 165 (I.i.2.9).

3. See "An Advertisement to the Reader," *Sancta Sophia*, pp. 549–50. The appendix was to have contained a "brief description of the nature, faculties, and operations of an intellectual soul."

4. Robert Burton calls it a "bare and razed table" in *Anatomy*, I, 166 (I.i.2.10). Cf. Baker's MS *Book D*, cited by Sitwell, *Holy Wisdom* (1964), p. xx.

5. For how man knows, see *Summa*, pp. 421–51 (Pt.I, QQ.84–88); for the active intellect, pp. 397–401 (Pt.I,Q.79,AA.2–5).

6. See *Summa*, pp. 408–12 (Pt.I,QQ.80–81).

7. *Summa*, p. 390 (Pt.I,Q.78,A.1). Burton calls these souls "facul-

ties," *Anatomy*, I, 155 (I.i.2.5), and refers to understanding and will as "powers."

8. *Commentary*, p. 177. See also *Sancta Sophia*, pp. 151–52 (1.3. 4.6), p. 533 (3.4.4.6). According to Pascal Parente, the term "center of the soul" was first employed by the Neoplatonist philosophers. "Plotinus speaks of a κέντρον ψυχῆς, the center or ground of the soul" (*Ennead*, VI.9,8); *The Mystical Life* (London, 1946), p. 43.

9. See St. Augustine's *Confessions*, pp. 203–23, or *de Trinitate*.

10. Watkin, *Philosophy of Mysticism*, p. 91.

11. St. Augustine, *Confessions*, pp. 207, 217–18, 220–21.

12. Martz, *The Paradise Within* (New Haven, 1964).

13. Aristotle, "Nichomachean Ethics," Bk.X:Ch.8:1178[b] in *The Basic Works of Aristotle*, ed. Richard McKeon (New York, 1941), p. 1107.

14. Dionysius, *The Mystical Theology*, i.3; cited by Christopher Dawson, *Progress and Religion* (New York, 1960), p. 131.

15. Merton College MS. 69, fol. 131b; cited by McCann in Baker, *Commentary*, pp. xiii–xiv.

16. Cited by E. I. Watkin, "Dom Augustine Baker," in *Great Catholics*, ed. Claude Williamson (New York, 1941), p. 185.

17. All cited by McCann in Baker, *Commentary*, p. xiv.

18. *Ibid.*, p. xiv; see also Aristotle, *Nic. Eth.*, 1139a, 32–35.

19. *Summa*, p. 1931 (Pt.II–II,Q.180,A.1).

20. *Summa*, p. 415 (Pt.I,Q.82,A.3).

21. Richard Hooker, *Of the Laws of Ecclesiastical Polity* (New York, 1907), I, 170 (I.vii.3). Where Hooker speaks of will apart from reason, it is will acting selfishly, willfully, or wrongly; e.g.: "Reason therefore may rightly discern the thing which is good, and yet the will of man not incline itself thereunto, as oft as the prejudice of sensible experience doth oversway"—*Ecclesiastical Polity*, I.vii.6; cited by Douglas Bush, *Paradise Lost in Our Time* (Cornell Univ. Press, 1945), p. 83n. The idea that the will may transcend natural reason rather than contradict it is one that I have not found in Hooker's works.

22. *Ibid.*, I, 102 (Preface.iii.10).

23. *Ibid.*, I, 176 (I.viii.3).

24. *Hobbes's Leviathan* (Oxford, 1909), pp. 46–47 (I.vi).

25. *Obscure Knowledge*, Ch. X. Cited by Watkin, *Philosophy*, pp. 97–98.

26. Knowles, *The English Mystics* (London, 1927), p. 164. Hereafter cited as *English Mystics* (1927).

27. *Confessions*, p. 43. As noted in Chapter 3, "exercise" need not be understood in an active sense: the word also describes experiences in which God is the agent.

28. Knowles, "Father Augustine Baker," p. 109. See also Sitwell, *Holy Wisdom* (1964), pp. viii–ix.

29. "The object of charity is the good, which is also the object of the will. Therefore charity is in the will as its subject." *Summa*, p. 1275 (Pt.II–II,Q.24,A.1).

30. St. Bernard, *On the Song of Songs*, trans. and ed. by a Religious of C.S.M.V. (London, 1952), p. 16; Hugh of St. Victor. *The Soul's Betrothal Gift*, trans. F. Sherwood Taylor (Westminster, 1945). p. 7.

31. See, for example, Edward Sapir, *Language* (New York, 1962), pp. 15–16.

32. *Inner Life*, I, 213. See also I, 240 and *Sancta Sophia* (1.3.4.11).

33. Baker, "Of that Mystic Saying 'Nothing and Nothing Make Nothing,'" appended to *Commentary* (1952 ed. only) p. 218.

34. See also *Sancta Sophia* (3.2.1.13).

35. St. Thomas: "In the present state of life in which the soul is united to a possible body, it is impossible for an intellect to understand anything actually, except by turning to the phantasms" (*Summa*, p. 429; Pt.I.Q.84,A.7). St. Thomas in this article, cites Aristotle: "the soul understands nothing without a phantasm" (*De Anima* iii.7). We have seen, though, that St. John of the Cross considers the use of imagery in prayer a step down from material reality.

36. E. I. Watkin, *Poets and Mystics*, pp. 219–22. Watkin argues that Baker's real opinion was that contemplation is imageless—a contention that I support. Gerard Sitwell, in *Holy Wisdom* (1964), pp. xix–xx, attributes these passages to Cressy's "nervousness" about Baker's orthodoxy on this point and cites a passage in Baker's *Book D* as a possible source. Sitwell says that Baker knew about imageless contemplation at second hand, "but that he did not grasp its significance"; this judgment, however, seems due to Baker's confusing and untraditional use of the terms "active" and "passive" in referring to contemplation (see previous chapter). Probably Baker thought that contemplation was imageless, but hesitated to contradict scholastic opinion. These passages remain, however, among the few instances of conflicting doctrines in *Sancta Sophia*.

37. *Summa*, pp. 286–87 (Pt.I,Q.57,A.4).

38. "Of Finding God Within Our Soul," p. 31.

39. Fr. Leander Jones, in "A Memorial," *Sancta Sophia* pp. 560–61, defends Baker on this point "although it be against the general doctrine of the Philosophers and Schoolmen."

40. St. John, *Works*, III, 110–14 (*Living Flame of Love*, I.9–14).

41. Hoopes, *Right Reason in the English Renaissance* (Cambridge, Mass., 1962), p. 161.

42. *Ibid.*, p. 5.

43. Howard Schultz, *Milton and Forbidden Knowledge* (New York, 1955), p. 72. See also pp. 27 and 246n.

44. Plato, *Republic* 518c, *Theatetus* 176b; cited by Hoopes, *Right Reason*, pp. 20–21.

45. *The Portable Renaissance Reader*, ed. J. B. Ross and M. M. McLaughlin (New York, 1961), p. 479.

46. Milton, "An Apology Against a Pamphlet," *Complete Prose Works of John Milton*, I, ed. Don M. Wolfe (New Haven, 1953), 890, 876.

47. *The Diary and Correspondence of Dr. John Worthington*, ed. Richard Christie, II, ii, Chetham Society, CXIV (1886), 322.

48. St. Ignatius, *Spiritual Exercises*, p. 37.

49. St. Thomas, *On the Truth of the Catholic Faith*, trans. and ed. Anton C. Pegis (New York, 1955), I, 67–68 (Bk.I,Ch.4).

Chapter Five

1. "An Advertisement to the Reader," *Sancta Sophia*, pp. 549–50.

2. McCann, "Some Benedictine Letters in the Bodleian," *Downside Review*, XLIX (1931), 466.

3. Robert Barclay, *An Apology for the True Christian Divinity* (London, 1678), pp. 256–57 (Prop. XI, Sect. 16). Cited by Charles Dodd [Hugh Tootel], *The Church History of England*, III (Brussels, 1742), 117.

4. Cf. Knowles, "Augustine Baker," p. 105; Watkin, "Dom Augustine Baker," p. 188; Higgins, "Augustine Baker," p. 163.

5. *Works*, I, 98–101 (*Ascent of Mt. Carmel*, II.xi.6–8).

6. See the relevant chapters in Fr. Knox's *Enthusiasm*.

7. See also *Sancta Sophia*, (1.3.8.10), and *Inner Life*, 217–18.

8. See Higgins, "Augustine Baker," p. 165. She cites from *Sancta Sophia*: knowledge of doctrines, p. 39; use of sacraments, pp. 67, 294, 346; submission to authority, p. 128.

9. Knowles, *The English Mystics* (1927), p. 165.

10. Cf. Higgins, "Augustine Baker," p. 171.

11. *St. Augustine's Enchiridion or Manual to Laurentius Concerning Faith, Hope, and Charity*, trans. and ed. Ernest Evans (London, 1933), p. 28.

12. St. John, *Works* III, 73 (*Living Flame of Love*, III.37).

13. *The Autobiography of Richard Baxter*, ed. J. M. Lloyd Thomas (London, 1931), pp. 106, 107.

14. Hooker, *Ecclesiastical Polity*, I, 135 (Pref.VIII.7); *The Journal of George Fox*, ed. Norman Penney (London, 1924), pp. 27–28.

15. Hughes, *A Popular History of the Catholic Church* (New York, 1954), p. 208.

16. Knox, *Enthusiasm*, pp. 134, 137–38.

17. It is clear from Fox's *Journal* that the Quakers made large inroads into the Seekers, Ranters, and other Nonconformists.

18. Fox's *Journal,* pp. 8–9.

19. Knox's *Enthusiasm,* p. 3.

20. Fox's *Journal,* p. 19.

21. Cited by Knox, *Enthusiasm,* pp. 114–15.

22. Baxter, *Autobiography,* p. 110.

23. Jeremy Taylor, *The Life of Our Blessed Lord,* Pt. I, Sect. 5, disc. 3. Cited by E. N. S. Thompson, "Mysticism in Seventeenth-Century English Literature," p. 219.

24. White, "Some Continuing Traditions," p. 969.

25. See David Mathew, *The Reformation and the Contemplative Life* (London, 1934).

26. See Howard Schultz, *Milton and Forbidden Knowledge* (New York, 1955), pp. 104–07 *et passim.*

27. Dodd, *Church History,* III, 117.

28. Knox, *Enthusiasm,* p. 7; Jones, *Spiritual Reformers in the Sixteenth and Seventeenth Centuries* (London, 1928), p. xiv; Baker, *The Wars of Truth,* p. 105.

Chapter Six

1. Henri Daniel-Rops, *The Church in the Seventeenth Century* (New York, 1965), I, 33.

2. James Broderick, S.J., *The Origin of the Jesuits* (New York, 1960), pp. 220–21. While the Jesuits are not a contemplative order, St. Ignatius may well be called a mystic.

3. Quoted by Daniel-Rops, *The Church in the Seventeenth Century,* I, 32.

4. Watkin, "Dom Augustine Baker," pp. 191, 175.

5. Knox, *Enthusiasm,* p. 240.

6. *Ibid.,* p. 3.

7. Watkin, *Philosophy of Mysticism,* p. 14.

8. *Inner Life,* 75; also *Sancta Sophia* (2.1.1.2).

9. See *The Catholic Encyclopedia,* 15 vols. (New York, 1907–14), s.v. "Theology, mystical."

10. See Chapter 7 for the view that Baker's prayer was not really mystical.

11. See *Inner Life,* I, 76–77, and *Confessions,* pp. 129–30.

12. Schmitz, *Histoire de l'Ordre de Saint-Benoît,* VI (Maredsous, 1949), 310; my translation. See also Paul Renaudin, *Quatre Mystiques Anglais* (Paris, 1945), pp. 125–26, 142.

13. Butler, *Benedictine Monachism,* pp. 35–45; Watkin, *Poets and Mystics* (London, 1953), p. 223.

Chapter Seven

1. George Bernanos, *The Diary of a Country Priest,* trans. Pamela Morris (New York, 1938), p. 103. Cited by Sister St. Teresa Higgins, "Augustine Baker," p. 17.

2. Thompson, "Mysticism in Seventeenth-Century English Literature," p. 171.

3. See *ibid.,* pp. 219–20, also Percy H. Osmond, *The Mystical Poets of the English Church* (London, 1919), pp. 101–11.

4. Benedictines of Stanbrook, *In a Great Tradition* (London, 1956), p. 24.

5. McCann, "Ten More Baker MSS," p. 79.

6. McCann, "Some Benedictine Letters in the Bodleian," p. 472.

7. *Ibid.,* p. 468.

8. McCann, Appendix II of Salvin and Cressy, *Lives,* p. 197.

9. See Benedictines of Stanbrook, *In a Great Tradition,* p. 20.

10. Schmitz, *Histoire de l'Ordre de Saint-Benoît,* VII, 333. My translation.

11. Guilday, *The English Catholic Refugees on the Continent, 1558–1795,* I (London, 1914), 278–79.

12. *The Diary of John Worthington,* ed. Christie, pp. 322–23.

13. Hugh Aveling, O.S.B., "The Catholic Recusancy of the Yorkshire Fairfaxes," *Recusant History,* IV (1957), 92; William Nicholls "Of the Rise and Progress of Spiritual Books of the Romish Church," in *An Introduction to a Devout Life . . . Translated and Reformed from the Errors of the Popish Edition* (London, 1701), n.p. (cited by by Helen C. White, *English Devotional Literature,* p. 111).

14. "An Advertisement to the Reader," *Sancta Sophia,* p. 550.

15. Joseph S. Hansom, ed., "The English Benedictine Nuns of the Convent of Our Blessed Lady of Good Hope in Paris . . . Notes and Obituaries," *Miscellenea VII,* Catholic Record Society, IX (London, 1911), 403. Cf. "Observe your own way, spirit and call" (*Commentary,* 154) and "*observe your call: which is all in all*; everyone according to the measure of his grace" (Salvin, 40).

16. Benedictines of Stanbrook, *In a Great Tradition,* p. 56.

17. *Ibid.,* pp. 75–76.

18. Abbot of Pershore, "Meditation and Contemplation," *Theology,* VI (1923), 216.

19. Underhill, *Mysticism* (New York, 1912), p. 559; Hodgson, *English Mystics* (Oxford, 1922), pp. 178–79.

20. Bush, *English Literature in the Earlier Seventeenth Century* (Oxford, 1962), p. 530; *Cambridge History of English Literature,* VII (Cambridge, Eng., 1911), 142–44.

21. Cuthbert Butler, *Benedictine Monachism* (Cambridge, Eng., 1961), pp. 104, 105.

22. For a discussion of this question see Butler's *Benedictine Monachism*, pp. 35–121; see also *The Rule of Saint Benedict*, trans. and ed. Justin McCann (London, 1952). Baker himself wrote a two-hundred-and-fifty-thousand-word treatise on the Rule.

23. For a fuller discussion, see Sister St. Teresa Higgins, "Augustine Baker," pp. 151–88.

24. There is a brief but significant objection to Knowles's interpretation of Baker in Thomas Merton's *Mystics and Zen Masters* (New York, 1967); Merton, himself a mystic, suggests that Knowles goes wrong by defining mysticism too narrowly.

25. Knowles, *The English Mystics* (1927), p. 176.

26. Knowles, "Father Augustine Baker," p. 109.

27. Knowles, *The English Mystics* (1927), pp. 168, 170.

28. Knowles, "Father Augustine Baker," p. 103.

29. Knowles, *The English Mystics* (1927), p. 173.

30. *Ibid.*, p. 153.

31. Knowles, "Father Augustine Baker," pp. 100, 101; see also Knowles, *The English Mystical Tradition* (New York, 1961), pp. 160, 173.

32. *Ibid.*, p. 103.

33. Sister St. Teresa Higgins, "Augustine Baker," *Dissertation Abstracts*, XXIV (1963), 2891.

34. Watkin, *Roman Catholicism in England from the Reformation to 1950*, p. 34.

35. White, *Tudor Books of Saints and Martyrs* (Madison, 1963), pp. 275–76.

36. Butler, "Dame Gertrude More," *Downside Review*, XXX (1911), 219.

37. Joseph Gillow, ed., *Miscellanea VIII*, Catholic Record Society, XIII (London, 1913), 81–82.

38. Jones, *Spiritual Reformers in the Sixteenth and Seventeenth Centuries*, p. xxiv.

Selected Bibliography

The bibliography lists most works by and about Baker, with the exception of book reviews and encyclopedia articles.

PRIMARY SOURCES

Acts and Affections for Mental Prayer. Ed. Dom Benedict Weld-Blundell. London: Sands and Co., 1931.

Apostolatus Benedictorium in Anglia . . . Opera et Industria R. P. Clementis Reyneri. Douay, 1626. This book, usually attributed to Clement Reyner, was assembled by Baker.

The Cloud of Unknowing . . . With a Commentary on the Cloud by Father Augustine Baker O.S.B. Ed. Dom Justin McCann. Westminster, Md.: Newman Press, 1952. The sixth, revised edition; first edition 1924.

The Confessions of Venerable Father Augustine Baker. Ed. Justin McCann. London: Burns, Oates & Washbourne, 1922. Baker's spiritual autobiography.

Contemplative Prayer, the Teaching of Ven. Augustine Baker Thereon. Ed. Dom B. Weld-Blundell. Exeter: Catholic Record Press, 1927. The first treatise of *Sancta Sophia*, with one chapter omitted.

Contemplative Prayer, Ven. Father Augustine Baker's Teaching Thereon. Ed. Dom B. Weld-Blundell. London, 1907. Abridgment of *Sancta Sophia*.

Custodia Cordis; a Treatise on Mortification. Rev. and ed. Dom Ildephonsus Cummins. St. Louis: B. Herder, 1907. Abridgment of the second treatise of *Sancta Sophia*.

Devotions of Dame Gertrude More. Rev. and ed. Reverend Henry Collins. London: n.p., 1873. Prayers from the appendix of *Sancta Sophia*, wrongly attributed.

The Divine Cloud, with Notes and a Preface by Father Augustin Baker, O.S.B. Ed. Reverend Henry Collins. London: Thomas Richardson and Sons, 1871.

Hail Jesus, or Acts upon the Life and Passion of Our Saviour Jesus Christ. By the Late Venerable Father F. Augustin Baker. London:

Burns & Oates, 1892. Part of the appendix of *Sancta Sophia* in tract form.

The Holy Practices of a Devine Lover; or the Sainctly Ideots Devotions. Paris: 1657. Selection of affective prayers attributed to Baker by Dom Justin McCann.

The Holy Practices of a Divine Lover, or the Saintly Idiot's Devotions. By Dame Gertrude More. Ed. Dom H. Lane Fox. London and Edinburgh: Sands & Co., 1909. Wrongly attributed to Dame Gertrude.

Holy Wisdom. Ed. Right Reverend Abbot Sweeney. New York: Harper, 1950.

Holy Wisdom; or Directions for the Prayer of Contemplation. Ed. Dom Gerard Sitwell. London: Burns & Oates, 1964. New edition; omits the preface and appendixes.

The Inner Life and the Writings of Dame Gertrude More. Rev. and ed. Dom Benedict Weld-Blundell. 2 vols. London: R. & T. Washbourne, 1910–11. Vol. I, an abridgment of Baker's life of Dame Gertrude; Vol. II, a modernized version of her *Spiritual Exercises* (1658), q.v.

Life of Dame Gertrude More . . . from Ancient MSS. Ed. Reverend Father [Henry] Collins. London: T. Richardson & Sons, 1877. Abridgment of Baker's MS, *More A.*

Memorials of Father Augustine Baker and Other Documents Relating to the English Benedictines. Ed. Dom Justin McCann and Dom Hugh Connolly, Catholic Record Society, Vol. XXXIII. London, 1933. Contains Baker's *Autobiography*, Pritchard's *Life*, part of Baker's mission treatise, a descriptive bibliography of Baker MSS, etc.

"Of Finding God Within Our Soul," *Downside Review*, LX (1942), 23–32. Contemplative treatise from MS collection (See Salvin and Cressy, 192).

Patterns of Devout Exercises. Ed. Dom B. Weld-Blundell. London, 1907. The appendix to Dom Weld-Blundell's *Contemplative Prayer* (q.v.) separately issued.

Prayer and Holiness. Ed. Dom Benedict Weld-Blundell. London: M. A. Magnani & Sons, 1933. Based on the Third Treatise of *Sancta Sophia.*

La Sainte Sapience, ou les voies de la prière contemplative. Intro. et notes par Jean Juglar, O.S.B. 2 vols. Paris: Editions d'Histoire et de Mystique, 1954.

Sancta Sophia. Or Directions for the Prayer of Contemplation &c. Extracted out of more than XL. Treatises written by the late Ven. Father F. Augustin Baker, a Monke of the English Congregation of the Holy Order of S. Benedict: And Methodically digested by

the R. F. Serenus Cressy, *Of the Same Order and Congregation. And printed at the Charges of his Conuent of S. Gregories, in Doway.* 2 vols. Douay: John Patte and Thomas Fievet, 1657.
Sancta Sophia, or Directions for the Prayer of Contemplation. New York: Edward Dunigan & Brother, 1857. Omits preface and appendixes.
Sancta Sophia, etc. Ed. by J. Norbert Sweeney. London: Burns, Oates & Washbourne, 1876. Frequently reprinted, the best modern text. The title is changed to *Holy Wisdom* in later printings.
Self-Discipline and Holiness, the Teaching of Ven. Augustine Baker Thereon. Ed. Dom B. Weld-Blundell. New York: P. J. Kenedy & Sons; London: Methuen, 1931. Second treatise of *Sancta Sophia,* less two chapters.

SECONDARY SOURCES

1. Works Concerned with Baker

ABBOT OF PERSHORE. "Meditation and Contemplation," *Theology,* VI (1923), 135–48, 205–18. Anglican approach to contemplation; discusses Baker pp. 214, 216.
ALLISON, A. F. "The 'Breve Compendio' in English," *Recusant History,* IV (1957–58), 4–17. Mentions Baker's treatise on the authorship of this work.
AVELING, HUGH, O.S.B. "The Catholic Recusancy of the Yorkshire Fairfaxes," *Recusant History,* IV (1957), 61–101. Mentions that Lady Abigail Fairfax, d. 1710, used *Sancta Sophia.*
[BAKER-GABB, RICHARD.] *The Families of Baker of Baily Baker and Baker Gabb, Abergavenny: a Memoir.* [Privately printed, 1903.] Family history and genealogy.
BARBANSON, CONSTANTINE. *The Secret Paths of Divine Love.* Introduction by Justin McCann. London: Burns, Oates & Washbourne, 1928. Part of this English version derives from Baker's MS. *Barbanson;* McCann discusses Baker, pp. vii–x.
BARCLAY, ROBERT. *An Apology for the True Christian Divinity, As the same is held forth, and preached by the People, Called, in Scorn, Quakers,* etc. Trans. [from Latin] Robert Barclay. London, 1678. Misquotes from *Sancta Sophia,* pp. 256–57.
BENEDICTINES OF STANBROOK. *In a Great Tradition.* London: John Murray, 1956. History of the English Benedictine nuns; comment on Baker.
BERLIERE, URSMER, O.S.B. "L'auteur de 'Sancta Sophia' Dom Augustin Baker, O.S.B.," *Revue liturgique et monastique,* XIII–XIV (1928–29), 281–89, 322–30, 370–85; 38–50. General introduction to Baker.

BIRT, DOM HENRY NORBERT. *Downside; the History of St. Gregory's School from Its Commencement at Douay to the Present Time.* London: K. Paul, Trench, Trübner and Co., 1902. Briefly mentions Baker.

BOLLAND, J., S.J. "The Psychology of Mental Prayer," *The Month,* CLXI O.S. (1933), 454–57. Article on Baker's method of prayer.

BRADNEY, JOSEPH ALFRED. *A History of Monmouthshire.* London: Mitchell, Hughes and Clarke, 1906. Discusses Baker, his life and family.

BUTLER, DOM CUTHBERT. *Benedictine Monachism; Studies in Benedictine Life and Rule.* Cambridge: Speculum Historiale, 1961. Discusses Baker, *passim.*

————. "Dame Gertrude More," *Downside Review,* XXX (1911), 219–23.

————. "Father Augustine Baker," *Downside Review,* LI (1933), 577–95. An examination of Bakerism.

————. *Western Mysticism.* London: Constable & Co., 1927. Useful introduction to mysticism, with valuable comments on Baker.

CHALLONER, BISHOP RICHARD. *Memoirs of Missionary Priests.* Ed. John Pollen. London: Burns, Oates & Washbourne, 1924. Discusses connection between Baker and Philip Powell.

"Collections Illustrating the History of the English Benedictine Congregation. Chapter VII," *The Rambler: A Catholic Journal and Review,* VII (1851), 214–16. Minor article on Baker.

CONNOLLY, DOM HUGH. "An Autograph Book of Father Augustine Baker," *Downside Review,* LXI (1943), 37–40. Discovery of an MS in Baker's handwriting.

————. "The Buckley Affair," *Downside Review,* XLIX (1931), 49–74. Discusses Baker's part in the aggregation, reproduces relevant documents.

————, ed. "Fr. Maihew on the Restoration of the English Congregation," *Downside Review,* L (1932), 490–97. Extracts from Maihew's *Trophaea* dealing with the Buckley affair.

[COOKE.] *Students Admitted to the Inner Temple, 1547–1660.* London: William Clowes and Sons, 1877. Transcription of Inner Temple records; Baker's matriculation, p. 146.

COWLEY, PATRICK. "Father Augustine Baker and the Sources of *Sancta Sophia,*" *Theology,* XXXVII (1938), 6–16. Source study.

CRESSY, DOM SERENUS. *The Church History of Brittany.* London, 1668. Makes some use of Baker's historical collections, Jesus College MSS. 75–78.

DE JAEGER, PAUL, S.J., ed. *Anthology of Mysticism.* Trans. Donald Atwater *et al.* Westminster, Md.: Newman Press, 1950. Selections from Baker on aspirations with a brief introduction, pp. 178–84.

DODD, CHARLES [HUGH TOOTELL]. *The Church History of England from the Year 1500, to the Year 1688. Chiefly with Regard to Catholics.* . . . 3 vols. Brussels: n.p., 1742. Article on "David Baker," III, 115–18.

ELLIS, HENRY. *Original Letters.* Vol. III. Second Series. London: Harding and Lepard, 1827. Baker's letter to Cotton.

ELLIS, T. P. *The Welsh Benedictines of the Terror.* Newtown, Wales: Welsh Outlook Press, 1936. From a Welsh nationalistic viewpoint; comments extensively on Baker.

"Father Augustine Baker: A Tercentenary," *Tablet,* CLXXVII (1941), 550. A brief notice.

"From Our Notebook," *Tablet,* CXCIV (1953), 224–25. Brief unsigned mention of Baker as part of the mystical tradition.

GILLOW, JOSEPH, ed. "Records of the Abbey of Our Lady of Consolation at Cambrai, 1620–1793," *Miscellanea VIII,* Catholic Record Society, XIII (London, 1913), 1–85.

GRIFFITH-DAVIES, J. D. "The Catholic Nonconformists of Monmouthshire," *The Monmouthshire Review,* II (1934), 29–45, 149–74. The second part is devoted to Baker.

GUILDAY, PETER. *The English Catholic Refugees on the Continent, 1558–1795.* London: Longmans, Green, 1914. Useful material on the founding of the English Benedictine abbeys in the Low Countries; some comment on Baker.

HANBURY, M. "New Light on Father Baker," *Pax,* XXIII (1933), 37–41. A brief notice.

HANSEN, SISTER MARY URBAN. "Dom Augustine Baker," *Benedictine Review,* III (1948), 28–32.

HANSOM, JOSEPH S. "The English Benedictine Nuns of the Convent of Our Blessed Lady of Good Hope in Paris. . . . Notes and Obituaries," *Miscellanea VII,* Catholic Record Society, IX (London, 1911), 334–431.

HAYNES, RENÉE. "Augustine Baker," *Month,* XXV (1961), 160–72. Mysticism in English Poetry as illuminated by Baker.

HEDLEY, BISHOP JOHN CUTHBERT. "Father Baker's *Sancta Sophia,*" *Dublin Review,* LXXIX (1876), 337–67. Also published as *Prayer and Contemplation* (1916), a Catholic Truth Society Tract; and in his *Evolution and Faith* (London: Sheed and Ward, 1931), pp. 163–206. Important commentary on Baker's approach to contemplation.

HIGGINS, SISTER M. ST. TERESA, C.S.J. "Augustine Baker," Unpublished doctoral dissertation, University of Wisconsin, 1963. A general study, with valuable comment on Baker and freedom; Baker and spirituality in women.

HODGSON, GERALDINE EMMA. *English Mystics.* London: Mowbray, 1922. Appreciation of Baker and Dame Gertrude More.

JUGLAR, JEAN. "La discretion selon Dom Baker," *Vie Spirituelle*, XC (1954), 401–19. Baker's moderation.

KNOWLES, DAVID. *The English Mystical Tradition.* London: Burns & Oates; New York, Harper & Brothers, 1961. Important study; critical of Baker and his doctrine (reprinted Harper Torchbooks, 1965).

——. *The English Mystics.* London: Burns, Oates & Washbourne, 1927. Earlier, more favorable view of Baker.

——. "English Spiritual Writers," *Clergy Review*, XLIII (1958), 641–57. Early version of his chapter on Baker in *The English Mystical Tradition* (1961).

——. "Father Augustine Baker." *English Spiritual Writers.* Ed. Charles Davis. New York: Sheed & Ward, 1962. Similar in tone and import to *The English Mystical Tradition.*

MACLEANE, DOUGLAS. *A History of Pembroke College Oxford.* Oxford: Oxford Historical Society, 1897. Brief life of Baker, pp. 130–31.

McCANN, DOM JUSTIN. "Augustine Baker: 'Directions for Contemplation,'" *Bodleian Quarterly Review*, V (1928), 219–20. Short note on Baker's life, on the occasion of the acquisition of this MS by the Bodleian Library, Oxford.

——. "Bakerism at Douay Seminary," *Clergy Review*, II (1931), 213–26.

——. "Dame Gertrude's Devotions," *Ampleforth Journal*, XXXIV (1929), 242–46. Companion article to "Father Baker's Devotions"; outlines D. Gertrude's writings.

——. "Father Baker on St. David," *Tablet*, CLXXXVII (1946), 113. Brief treatise on the patron saint of Wales, Baker's namesake, with a short introduction by McCann.

——. "Father Baker's Dame Gertrude," *Downside Review*, XLVII (1929), 157–67. Discusses Baker's treatise on Gertrude More.

——. "Father Baker's Devotions," *Ampleforth Journal*, XXXIV (1929), 135–50. Baker's affective prayers in the *Ideots Devotions* (1657).

——. "Father Baker's Tercentenary," *Downside Review* LIX (1941), 355–71. Discusses Baker as mystic.

——. "Some Benedictine Letters in the Bodleian," *Downside Review*, XLVIII–XLIX (1930–31), 465–81. Efforts to suppress Bakerism by Fr. Claude White.

——. "Ten More Baker MSS.," *Ampleforth Journal*, LXIII (1958), 77–83. Supplementary bibliography.

——. *Revue d'Ascetique et de Mystique*, LVII (1934), 102. Untitled extract from Baker's *Directions for Contemplation* (Ampleforth Abbey MS, p. 33), on a meeting between Dom Placid Gascoigne and Constantine Barbanson.

McCANN, DOM JUSTIN AND DOM COLUMBA CARY-ELWES, eds. *Ampleforth and Its Origins; Essays on a Living Tradition by Members of the Ampleforth Community.* London: Burnes, Oates & Washbourne, 1952. Chapter on Baker by McCann.

McLAUGHLIN, J. B., O.S.B. "Dame Gertrude More, Contemplative (1606–1653)," *Month,* CLI (1923), 119–26. Also discusses Baker.

MERTON, THOMAS. *Mystics and Zen Masters.* New York: Farrar, Straus and Giroux, 1967; Delta Books, 1969. Essay on Baker and Dame Gertrude More; brief critique of Knowles.

MORE, DAME GERTRUDE. *The Spiritual Exercises of the Most Vertuous and Religious D. Gertrude More.* Ed. Fr. Francis Gascoigne. Paris: L. de la Fosse, 1658. Based on Baker's collection of D. Gertrude's writings, *Confessiones Amantis.*

MOUSTIER, BENOÎT DU. "Spiritual Direction According to Father Baker," *Spiritual Life,* IV (1958), 205–12. Baker's belief in spiritual liberty, flexible direction.

NICHOLLS, WILLIAM, ed. *St. Francis de Sales, An Introduction to the Devout Life . . . Translated and Reformed from the Errors of of the Popish Edition,* etc. London: E. Holt, 1701. Mentions *Sancta Sophia* in the introduction.

POULAIN, A., S.J. *The Graces of Interior Prayer,* trans. Leonora L. Yorke Smith. London: Kegan Paul, Trench, Trübner & Co., 1912. Mentions Baker p. 105; a good general work on mysticism.

POURRAT, PIERRE. *Christian Spirituality.* Trans. W. H. Mitchell. 4 vols. Westminster, Md.: Newman Press, 1922–55. Brief note on Baker, IV, 436–37.

RÄSS, BISHOP ANDREAS. *Die Convertiten seit der Reformation, nach ihrem Leben und aus ihren Schriften dargestellt.* 13 bde. und Register. Freiburg im Breisgau, 1866–80. Commentary on Baker, II, 100–122.

[REEVE, DOM WILFRED.] "An Account of the Venerable Fr. Augustine Baker," *Ampleforth Journal,* IV (1898), 59–74, 196–213. The Life and writings of Baker, supplied by Dom Reeve about 1691 to Anthony Wood, used in the second edition of *Athenae Oxonienses* (1721).

RENAUDIN, PAUL. "L'autobiographie d'un mystique anglais: Dom Baker," *Vie Spirituelle,* LIII (1938), 280–98 and LIV (1939), 39–63. Superseded by *Quatre Mystiques Anglais.*

———. *Quatre Mystiques Anglais; Richard Rolle, Juliane de Norwich, Dom Augustin Baker, Gertrude More.* Paris: Editions du Cerf, 1945. Rather critical view of Baker.

Ruiz, S., O.S.B. "Doctrina espiritual de la oración V. Dom Baker," *Vie Spirituelle*, XXIX (1932), 371–79.

——. "Doctrina espiritual del V.P. Dom Augustín Baker," *Vida Sobrenatural*, XXVII–XXVIII (1933), 161–68, 225–34.

Salvin, Dom Peter, and Dom Serenus Cressy. *The Life of Father Augustine Baker, O.S.B. (1575–1641)*. Ed. Dom Justin McCann. London: Burns, Oates & Washbourne, 1933. Includes McCann's useful introductory essays and his registers of Baker MSS and published books.

Schmitz, Dom Philibert. *Histoire de l'Ordre de Saint-Benoit*. 7 vols. Maredsous: Les Editions de Maredsous, 1942–56. Good general history with some discussion of Baker.

Sitwell, Dom Gerard, ed. Walter Hilton, *The Scale of Perfection*. London: Burns & Oates, 1953. Brief comment on Baker, pp. xv–xvi.

Snow, Abbot Terence B. *Obit Book of the English Benedictines from 1600 to 1912*. Revised by Dom Henry Norbert Birt. Edinburgh: J. C. Thomson, 1913.

Sweeney, Abbot J[ames] Norbert. *The Life and Spirit of Father Augustine Baker*. London: n.p., 1861. Only full biography; dated by later discoveries.

Taunton, Reverend Ethelred L. *The English Black Monks of St. Benedict; A Sketch of their History*. 2 vols. London: John C. Nimmo, 1897. Discusses Baker.

Underhill, Evelyn. *Mysticism*. New York: E. P. Dutton, 1912. Comments on Baker.

Ward, A. W., and A. R. Waller, eds. *The Cambridge History of English Literature*. 15 vols. Cambridge: Cambridge University, 1907–27. W. H. Hutton discusses Baker, VII, 142–44.

Watkin, E[dward] I[ngram]. "Dom Augustine Baker." *Great Catholics*. Ed. Claude Williamson. New York: Macmillan, 1941. Baker as a reliable spiritual guide.

——. "Father Baker and Active Contemplation," *Downside Review*, LXIII (1945), 102–24. Supersedes his "A Note on Contemplation" (q.v.).

——. "A Note on Contemplation," *Downside Review*, LX (1942), 299–308. On Baker's "active" contemplation and union.

——. *Poets and Mystics*. London: Sheed & Ward, 1953. A valuable chapter on Baker supersedes the three articles above.

Webb, W. K. L., S.J. "Thomas Preston O.S.B., alias Roger Widdrington (1567–1640)," *Biographical Studies* II (1954), 216–68. That Baker's superior in England, Dom Preston, advised him to take the Oath before the arrival of the papal prohibition.

Weldon, Dom Bennet. *Chronological Notes . . . of the Order of St.*

Benedict. Ed. Dom Gilbert Dolen. London: John Hodges, 1881.

WHITE, HELEN C. *Tudor Books of Saints and Martyrs.* Madison: University of Wisconsin, 1963. Brief mention of Baker.

WOOD, ANTHONY. *Athenae Oxonienses.* Second edition. London: Knaplock, 1721. Article on "David Baker" with important list of Baker MSS, some of which have not survived, II, 3–9. See under Dom Wilfred Reeve, above.

WORTHINGTON, JOHN. *The Diary and Correspondence of Dr. John Worthington.* Ed. Richard Copley Christie. Vol. II, Pt. 2. Chetham Society, Vol. CXIV. Manchester, 1886. Contains his letter to Henry More about Baker.

2. Useful Background Material

AUGUSTINE, SAINT. *The Confessions of Saint Augustine.* Trans. Edward B. Pusey. New York: Random House, 1949. Basic work of Western spirituality.

BAKER, HERSCHEL. *The Wars of Truth.* Cambridge: Harvard University Press, 1952. Useful intellectual background.

BAXTER, RICHARD. *The Autobiography of Richard Baxter.* Ed. J. M. Lloyd Thomas. Everyman Edition. London: J. M. Dent, 1931. Moderate Presbyterian viewpoint.

BENEDICT, SAINT. *The Rule of Saint Benedict.* Trans. and ed. Abbot Justin McCann. London: Burns Oates, 1952.

BURTON, ROBERT. *The Anatomy of Melancholy.* Ed. Holbrook Jackson. 3 vols. London: J. M. Dent, 1932. Compendium of Elizabethan opinion.

FOX, GEORGE. *The Journal of George Fox.* Ed. Norman Penney. London: J. M. Dent, 1924. Religious experiences of Quaker founder.

GERARD, JOHN. *The Autobiography of a Hunted Priest.* Trans. Philip Caraman. New York: Doubleday, 1955. Background of Elizabethan persecution of Catholics.

GILLOW, JOSEPH. *A Literary and Biographical History, or Biographical Dictionary, of the English Catholics.* 5 vols. London: Burns and Oates, 1885–1902. Short biographies of Baker and many of those connected with him.

HAVRAN, MARTIN J. *The Catholics in Caroline England.* Stanford: Stanford University Press, 1962. Reliable study.

HILTON, WALTER. *The Scale of Perfection.* Trans. Leo Sherley-Price. London: Penguin Books, 1957. Medieval English mystic; important influence on Baker.

HOBBES, THOMAS. *Hobbes's Leviathan.* Oxford: Clarendon Press, 1909. Seventeenth–century materialist and skeptic.

HOOKER, RICHARD. *Of the Laws of Ecclesiastical Polity.* 2 vols. New York: E. P. Dutton, 1907. The Anglican position.

HUGHES, FATHER PHILIP. *Rome and the Counter-Reformation in England.* London: Burns and Oates, 1942. Useful study.

IGNATIUS DE LOYOLA, SAINT. *The Spiritual Exercises of St. Ignatius.* Trans. Anthony Mottola. Intro. Robert W. Gleason. New York: Doubleday, 1964. Most influential religious work of Counter-Reformation.

JOHN OF THE CROSS, SAINT. *The Complete Works of Saint John of The Cross; Doctor of the Church.* Trans. and ed. E. Allison Peers. Three volumes in one. Westminster, Md.: Newman Press, 1964. Authoritative work on mysticism.

JONES, RUFUS MATTHEW. *Spiritual Reformers in the Sixteenth and Seventeenth Centuries.* London: Macmillan, 1928. Thoughtful if impressionistic study.

JULIAN OF NORWICH, DAME. *Revelations of Divine Love.* Ed. Roger Huddleston. Westminster, Md.: Newman Press, 1952. Medieval English mystic, known to Baker.

KNOX, R[ONALD] A. *Enthusiasm; A Chapter in the History of Religion with Special Reference to the XVII and XVIII Centuries.* Oxford: Clarendon Press, 1950. Most useful history of religious enthusiasm.

LEJEUNE, ABBÉ P. *An Introduction to the Mystical Life.* Trans. Basil Levett. London, R. & T. Washbourne, 1915. Lucid exposition.

LEYS, M[ARY] D. R. *Catholics in England 1559–1829: A Social History.* London: Longmans, Green, 1961. Useful background.

MARTZ, LOUIS L. *The Poetry of Meditation.* New Haven: Yale University Press, 1962. Effect of meditative Prayer on English poetry.

PEERS, E[DGAR] ALLISON. *Studies of the Spanish Mystics.* 3 vols. London: S.P.C.K., 1951–60. Standard work.

RENAUDIN, PAUL. *Un Maître de la Mystique français Benoît de Canfeld.* Paris, 1956. Baker's fellow English mystic.

TERESA OF AVILA, SAINT. *The Complete Works of Saint Teresa of Jesus.* Trans. and ed. E. Allison Peers. 3 vols. London: Sheed & Ward, 1944–46. Basic mystical writings.

THOMAS AQUINAS, SAINT. *Summa Theologica.* Trans. Fathers of the English Dominican Province. 3 vols. New York: Benziger Brothers, 1946–48.

THOMPSON, ELBERT N. S. "Mysticism in Seventeenth-Century English Literature," *Studies in Philology,* XVIII (1921), 170–231. Broad, useful study.

WATKIN, E[DWARD] I[NGRAM]. *The Philosophy of Mysticism.* London: Grant Richards, 1920. A good introduction.

WHITE, HELEN C. *English Devotional Literature 1600–1640.* Madison: University of Wisconsin, 1931. Standard survey.

———. "Some Continuing Traditions in English Devotional Literature," *Publications of the Modern Language Association of America,* LVII (1942), 966–80. Anglican adoption of Catholic spirituality; decay of English mysticism.

Index